Sustainable Animal Production from Small Farm Systems in South-East Asia

by
C. Devendra
Senior Programme Officer
Animal Production System (Asia)
International Development Research Centre (IDRC)
Singapore

Published by arrangement with the Food and Agriculture Organization of the United Nations
by
Daya Publishing House®
A Division of
Astral International Pvt. Ltd.
New Delhi - 110 002

First Indian Edition, 1998
Reprinted, 2016
ISBN: 978-81-7035-213-6

Published by : **Daya Publishing House®**
A Division of
Astral International Pvt. Ltd.
– ISO 9001:2008 Certified Company –
4760-61/23, Ansari Road, Darya Ganj
New Delhi-110 002
Ph. 011-43549197, 23278134
E-mail: info@astralint.com
Website: www.astralint.com

Printed at : **Chawla Offset Printers,**
Delhi-110052

Contents

CORRIGENDA

FAO Animal Production and Health Paper No. 106 – 1993
Sustainable animal production from small farm systems in South-East Asia

103	The N production figure for chicken should be 1.95 g and for ducks 1.80 g
137	Appendix 3: (MT) is to replace (kg/yr) in all titles for Tables 1 to 7

M-21/T0757E/2.93/1500
ISSN 0254-6019
ISBN 92-5-103168-1

Foreword

Food production results from the interaction of human, animal, land, water and capital resources. In many farming systems of the developing countries animals have an integral role and the full range of animal products are utilized. Many of these outputs are also important farm inputs, such as, manure and draught power. Animals also provide a strategic source of cash which can be called on as required to purchase other essential farm inputs and food during the critical periods of the year, thus helping to alleviate poverty and increase household food security. With an increasing world population, food production cannot be allowed to stagnate, clearly, there is a need for more sustainable increases in agricultural output. The complementarity between crops and livestock, which allows for nutrient recycling, energy and value added production is unique and needs fully exploiting. FAO has attached the highest priority to sustainable development of both plants and animal agriculture in its programmes. The Animal Production and Health Division (AGA) of FAO has instigated a number of case studies examining aspects of sustainability in the different agro-ecological zones and the major animal production systems in the world. This publication examines the role of animal production in the small farm systems in South-East Asia.

Final editing and formating of the publication was undertaken by **A.W. Speedy**, Department of Plant Sciences, University of Oxford, England.

Executive summary

CHAPTER 1
Introduction

This introductory chapter provides the background to the importance of small farms in Asian agriculture, the generally low level of efficiency and the problems of resource degradation, competition for land for alternative enterprises, decreasing investment in livestock development by international agencies and inadequate demonstration of the role of animals in the development of sustainable agriculture. Human population increase and the overriding demand for food will be awesome and will increase pressure on the use of natural resources. A conceptual framework for the development of crop-animal systems is given.

The chapter emphasizes the aim of the publication: to assess the opportunities for increasing the current contribution made by animals to improved efficiency in the management and use of natural resources, demonstration of low-input integrated farming systems, alleviation of rural poverty and sustainable production that has economic, ecological and sociological benefits.

The focus of the publication is on South-East Asia, made up essentially of those countries in Indo-China and the Association of South-East Asian Nations (ASEAN): Brunei Darussalam, Cambodia, Indonesia, Laos, Malaysia, Myanmar, Philippines, Singapore, Thailand and Vietnam.

CHAPTER 2

The small farm scenario

South-East Asia presents an overwhelming panorama of small farms with large populations of small farmers and peasants who own both ruminants and non-ruminants. The small farm scenario, which includes small farm systems and small farmers, is described in detail. The key elements in a definition of small farms are subsistence, low income and illiteracy. Of the land area available of 434 million ha, only 17.8% is under arable and permanent crops, and 3.7% is permanent pasture. The ratio is about 0.96 ha/person. The average size of small farms is 1-2 ha. The density of ruminant livestock populations is highest in Asia, compared to Africa and Latin America.

The evolutionary phases in integrated crop-animal systems is given. Three types of small farms are identified: farms in rain-fed agriculture, farms in irrigated agriculture and farms in plantation agriculture. Within these, two types of integrated systems exist: systems combining crops, non-ruminants, ponds and fish, and systems combining crops and ruminants. Eight major advantages of integrated systems are given.

Characteristics of small farms (small size, crop-animal systems, low input use, low level of economic efficiency and diversification) and small farmers (low income, continual exposure to hunger and poverty, resistance to change, illiteracy and lack of interest in extension materials, but capacity to adapt and survive hardship, secure tenure and rational use of limited resources) are given. Gender issues are introduced, including the fact that women work longer than men and children are involved in livestock management.

CHAPTER 3

Animal resources

Animal populations in South-East Asia, as percentages of world populations, are approximately 13% of the buffaloes, 3% of the cattle, 3% of goats, 0.6% of sheep, 18% of ducks, 10% of poultry and 5% of the pigs. Approximately 76-95% of the different species populations are owned by small farmers. The number of small ruminants is increasing faster (3.6-4.1% *per annum*) than large ruminants. The highest growth rate was achieved by poultry at 9.1%. The average livestock share of agricultural and total GDP were 12.3 and 2.9% respectively. The significance of animal ownership is described. Several important indigenous breeds are identified and a classification of animal-based systems is given.

Ruminant production systems are in three categories (extensive systems, systems combining arable cropping and systems integrated with tree cropping). It is suggested that the future nature of ruminants production systems is unlikely to change. However, shifts within the systems will occur through intensification.

CHAPTER 4

Contribution to food production

The contribution to food production includes meat, milk and eggs. Of the total meats produced, pig meat accounted for 44.3%, poultry meat 33.0%, beef and veal 11.9%, buffalo meat 5.5%, duck meat 2.9%, goat meat 1.6% and mutton and lamb 0.8%. The growth rates for total meat production, total milk and poultry eggs were 3.7%, 4.2% and 4.8% *per annum* respectively. Considerable variation exists in *per capita* dietary energy and protein intakes.

CHAPTER 5

The feed resource base

The feed resource base is discussed with reference to forages, crop residues, agro-industrial by-products and non-conventional feeds. The total quantity of cereal straw and agro-industrial by-products from field and tree crops was 219 million tonnes in 1989, of which about 70 million tonnes or 32% are considered to be non-conventional. Constraints to feed utilization are discussed, including low digestibility, low protein content and toxic principles. Published information on nutritive value is available in all countries.

The advantages of integrating ruminants with tree crops and the value of multi-purpose trees is described.

The importance of strategic supplementation to create an efficient rumen ecosystem and balance the products of digestion with by-pass nutrients of dietary origin is emphasized. Priorities for feed resource use are indicated, including examples of primary feeds for intensive use in different countries.

CHAPTER 6

Major constraints on production

Major constraints to production are enumerated and discussed. These include size of farms, growth in illiteracy and urbanization, as well as institutional rigidity and too much emphasis on commodity-focused research. Attention is given to forage production, animal breeding, animal health, common property rights, support services, market outlets and manpower training.

Individual constraints are discussed in detail and, in some cases, solutions are proposed. Thus, for example, constraints to organized animal breeding on small farms is considered with three alternative approaches: selection within indigenous breeds, importation of breeds for crossing and importation of improved breeds.

Particular emphasis is given to the importance of the systems approach (stages, natural resources, participatory research and development, eco-regional relevance, inter-disciplinary research, monitoring and feedback). Experiences and lessons learnt about systems research in Asia are described. The latter include improved land use systems, gender effects, stability, sustainability, institutional support, farmer participation, shift from cropping systems to crop-animal systems and impact analysis.

CHAPTER 7

Potentially important sustainable technologies

Potentially important sustainable technologies in South East Asia are identified and reviewed in detail. These involve both annual cropping systems and tree cropping systems. Within the former are food-feed intercropping, relay cropping, the three strata forage system, crop-animal systems in lowland rain-fed areas, integrated animal-fish-crops systems and systems combining crops and animals.

Practical benefits of supplementation, processing and all year round feeding systems are reviewed. Utilization of research results at the small farm level, phases in on-farm research and large scale on-farm testing are also discussed. The latter includes information needed by farmers and their advisers, mechanisms for the delivery of information to farmers and criteria for development orientation. Potential levels of productivity that can be achieved through the development of sustainable systems is illustrated.

CHAPTER 8

The development of integrated systems

The development of integrated systems is discussed with reference to the pig-ducks-fish-vegetable sequence, integration involving various animals, significance of manure from animals, productivity of fish, and future of integrated systems involving ponds. The latter is limited by several factors such as inadequate land, feed availability and access to ponds.

Integrated small ruminants-tree cropping systems remain to be fully developed together with an appropriate methodology. In the case of small ruminants, there are effects of animal integration on the parent crop as well as of the crop on the animal. Attention is drawn to the advances being made in integrated systems based on sugar cane. There is a general paucity of knowledge on integrated systems which justifies research and development to demonstrate their potential value.

CHAPTER 9

The framework for development of integrated systems

The framework for the development of integrated systems is addressed in detail. This includes criteria for project formulation, resource requirements, institutional requirements, policy support, implementation, criteria for evaluation and impact analysis. The conservation of on-farm genetic bio-diversity is accorded a high priority.

Several criteria for project formulation are listed (e.g., national and regional development goals and requirements for the alleviation of poverty and sustainability of the system). Criteria for evaluation include cost-benefit analysis, before-and-after trends and environmental accounting. Impact analysis involves the direct effects on households and indirect benefits of the research.

CHAPTER 10

Conclusions

The concluding chapter reiterates the continuing importance of small farm systems combining crops and animals in South-East Asia. The challenging task is that of linking sustainability to agricultural growth and the alleviation of poverty. For animal production, the challenges and expectations will be even greater, in view of concerns about their current contribution. An increased contribution from animals in the future needs to be identified with their ecological and socio-economic impact.

The development of sustainable integrated small farm systems using a systems approach will require more intensive and complex methodologies, greater farmer participation, awareness of increased environmental concerns and continuous monitoring of the sustainability of the systems.

Chapter 1
Introduction

THE SIGNIFICANCE OF SMALL FARMS

Small farm systems constitute an integral part of Asian agriculture. These systems, which are labour-intensive and combine animals with mixed cropping, vary between regions and Asia presents, by any standard, a preponderance of small farms and a complexity of production systems that is unique to the region. This type of farm forms the backbone of food production in all countries and therefore constitutes an important target area for research and development.

The complex systems utilize draught power from animals, produce crops for home use, sale and animal feed, and also provide animal products for domestic consumption and commercial sale. Crops and animals thus play an important complementary role in the use of the available natural resources and the achievement of self-sufficiency with respect to feed, fertiliser and the requirement for human food. These mixed activities contribute significantly towards the stability of farm households and self-reliance.

Although the importance of small farms in food production is widely reccgnized, questions and doubts have emerged about their efficiency and especially the contribution made by animals. National targets for animals proteins, relative to the contribution from crops, are far from being realized, which in turn has raised further doubts about the efficiency of existing production systems and the utilization of resources to support these systems. Additionally, these aspects are exacerbated by a number of associated concerns which include *inter alia*:

- resource degradation and environmental damage caused by deforestation and overgrazing;
- competition for land for alternative enterprises;
- contribution to global warming (carbon dioxide and methane);
- inadequate technology transfer or demonstration of how livestock can play a key role in the development of sustainable agriculture in different agro-ecosystems; and
- decreasing investments in livestock projects by such agencies as the World Bank and the Asian Development Bank.

POPULATION INCREASE AND DEMAND FOR FOOD

The overriding problem is population increase which is greater in absolute terms than in any other region. It is estimated that the population in Asia will grow from 2.6 billions in 1985 to 4.4 billions in 2025. Within this, South-East Asia alone will account for a projected increase to 2.3 billion, equivalent to 52% of the total. In this context, malnutrition and abject poverty will be continuing concerns.

The magnitude of the latter is reflected in Table 1.1, published by the World Bank (1992) and based on data by Ravallion *et al.* (1992). The table illustrates that, in 1985, about 65% of the total estimated number of 714 millions poor people were found in Asia. Of this, 13.2% or 182 million were found in South-East Asia. By contrast, in East Asia, the projections for the year 2000 suggest that the percentage of the population below the poverty line will decrease to 4.2%, corresponding to 73 million poor people.

The combined maladies of poverty and awesome population growth clearly emphasise the importance of increasing food production. They determine the demand for animal products in terms of both quantity and quality. Together with income growth and increasing urbanisation, these will also determine the composition of food demand.

The task of producing more food in Asia will therefore increase the pressure on the natural resource base and determine how it must be managed and used. As it is, serious environmental problems have already arisen. Rapid industrialization and urbanization have resulted in chronic air and water pollution. In the rural areas, rapidly increasing populations have led to increased pressures on the use of limited and decreasing natural resources: increased fuelwood demand, further deforestation and deterioration of soil quality.

Table 1.1 The extent of poverty (World Bank, 1992)

Region	Percentage of population below the poverty line*			Number of poor (millions)		
	1985	1990	2000	1985	1990	2000
South Asia	51.8	49.0	36.9	532	562	511
East Asia	13.2	11.3	4.2	182	169	73
Sub-Saharan Africa	47.6	47.8	49.7	184	216	304
Middle East and North Africa	30.6	33.1	30.6	60	73	89
Eastern Europe**	7.1	7.1	5.8	5	5	4
Latin America and the Caribbean	22.4	25.5	24.9	87	108	126
All developing countries	30.5	29.7	24.1	1051	1133	1107

* Set at US$370 annual income.

** Does not include the former USSR.

The focus on more efficient management and use of natural resources is justified by the two urgent priorities of the 1990's: reduction of poverty and protection of the environment. These two critical components will thus have to be simultaneously addressed through strategies that can ameliorate the situation.

The response to the need for increased food production was achieved in the 1950's through the Green Revolution with impressive increases in cereal production, although the benefits were mainly confined to the irrigated lowlands of Asia. In the four decades since then, economic development has been associated with the redistribution of wealth and meeting the basic needs of the poor, such as nutrition, education and sanitation. During this time, there has been a considerable impact on prosperity and standards of living. Social indicators like life expectancy at birth, infant mortality rate, primary school enrolments and anthropometric measures of malnutrition further reflect the improvements made. These trends have led to the world food supply now being demonstrably adequate and the remaining problem is one of distribution of the available resources (Anderson, 1991).

THE DEVELOPMENT OF CROP-ANIMAL SYSTEMS

Efforts to maximise the productivity of crop-animal systems need to consider the natural resource base, as well as the socio-economic environment, in the context of the objectives of development and the targets to be achieved. Figure 1 provides a conceptual framework and the broad relationships between these factors.

Figure 1. Sustainable crop-animal systems in Asia.

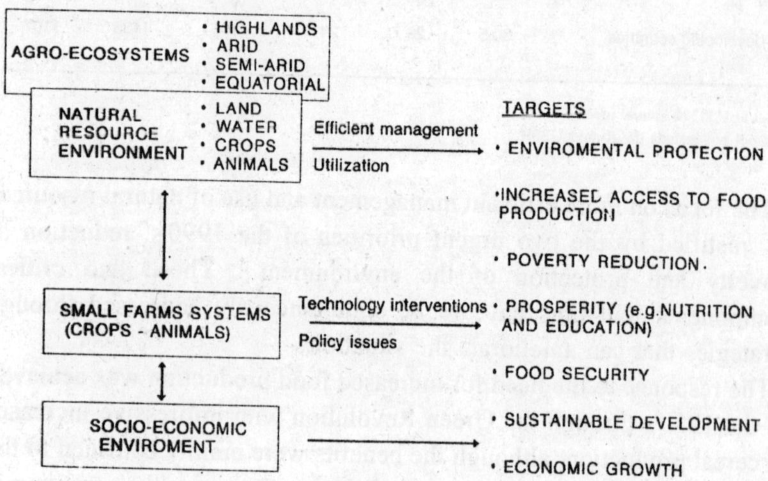

The more formidable task is that of translating the concept into strategies for action at the farm level. These strategies need to focus specifically on crop-animal systems which involve community participation of farm households and to directly address both production, post-production and consumption systems. Central to this development and wider application of potentially important technologies is on-farm research and development and, in particular, the utilization of research results (Devendra and Chantalakhana, 1992).

A strategy for the development of sustainable crop-animal system must therefore consider the following issues:

- integrated systems and improved efficiency in the use and management of natural resources;
- demonstration of environmentally sound, low-input integrated farming systems;
- strategies that can concurrently promote alleviation of rural poverty, attainment of food security, as well as meeting the needs and stability of farming families; and
- the formulation of strategic options and an operational framework for more sustainable production while, at the same time, providing economic, ecological and sociological benefits.

PURPOSE OF THE PUBLICATION

In these circumstances, it is appropriate to examine and assess the current contribution of animals to small farm systems and potential opportunities for increasing the level of production and developing strategies that can make these systems more sustainable. These aspects will be considered with specific reference to South-East Asia which is essentially made up of those countries in Indo-China and the Association of South-East Asian Nations (ASEAN): Brunei Darussalam, Cambodia, Indonesia, Laos, Malaysia, Myanmar, Philippines, Singapore, Thailand and Vietnam.

Chapter 2

The small farm scenario

DEFINITION OF SMALL FARMS

A number of definitions have been proposed to describe both small farmers and small farms. Adams and Coward (1972) referred to a small farmer as one who had very little access to political power, productive assets and/or income streams within society. FAO/RAFE (1978) defined small farmers, small fishermen and peasants in broad terms, including the low-income producers of agricultural, livestock and aquatic products. They referred, in particular, to tenants, informal tenants such as share croppers, landless agricultural labourers and small owner-operators. Wapenham (1979) defined a small farmer as an agricultural producer controlling no more land than he can farm without the permanent employment of non-family labour. Steenwinkel (1979) included in his definition all people in the rural areas of developing countries who do not have the means to provide for their basic needs or are living in constant fear of losing their means. The key elements in all of these definitions are subsistence, low income and illiteracy.

Small farms have been defined as household units that make most management decisions, control most of the farm labour supply and normally much of the capital as well. Since the family and the farm unit are the same, labour and capital expenditure decisions represent a choice between household and farm considerations. A more precise definition of small farms is that they are complex interrelationships between animals, crops and farming families, involving small land holdings and minimum resources of labour and capital, from which small farmers may or may not be able to derive a regular and adequate supply of food or an acceptable income and standard of living.

Irrespective of the definition used, the important point is that Asia presents an overwhelming panorama of small farms with large populations of small farmers and peasants owning both ruminant and non-ruminant animals.

THE SMALL FARM ENVIRONMENT

Climatic factors

The countries in South-East Asia fall within the equatorial climate zone, stretching from 5° to 7° latitude north and south of the equator, characterized by a constant high temperature and high humidity. Rainfall is abundant (2000-3000 mm) and, although roughly distributed throughout the year, tends to be heavier during some parts of the year and lighter at other times. In general, animals in this climate tend to be smaller in size due to the effects of humidity on growth rates.

The high temperature and rainfall favours vigorous plant growth. Forage production is relatively easy and available all the year round. The main problem however is one of the control of growth to ensure that forages do not become too mature, i.e. too fibrous, and that they have a good nutritive value when fed to animals.

Intensive crop production produces abundant fibrous crop residues which are potentially important to the nutrition of herbivores. Additionally, and with specific reference to trees or perennial crops like coconuts, oil palm and rubber, there exists considerable native undergrowth and an abundance of shade which is advantageous especially for exotic animals introduced into this zone. One serious disadvantage of this climate is that the high humidity and rainfall favours internal and external parasites which, if uncontrolled, can be a major constraint to animal production.

Land use

The extent of land available and the categories of land are given in Table 2.1. Out of the total available land area of 434 million hectares, forests and woodlands (land under natural or planted stands of trees) accounted for 52%, followed by other land: 26% (built in areas, roads, barren lands, etc.), arable and permanent crop land: 17.8% and permanent pasture: 3.7%. The area of land is about 0.96 ha/person.

Table 2.1 Land use in South-East Asia (FAO, 1990)

Type of land use	Area (million ha)	% of total	Ruminant livestock units (millions)*
Arable land and permanent crops	77.7	17.8	
Permanent pasture	15.9	3.7	373
Forest and woodland	225.5	52.0	
Other land	114.9	26.5	
Total land area	434.0	100.0	

* Conversion factors: buffalo=1.0, cattle=0.8, goats and sheep=0.1

Unlike Latin America, most grazing land in South-East Asia is permanent pasture. This limitation reinforces the importance of integrated crop-animal systems and the role of animals within these systems. Attention is drawn however to the availability of about 226 million ha of land under forests and woodland, which includes the area under tree crops (e.g., coconuts, oil palm and rubber). This area, especially the herbage under tree crops, is essentially unused and represents a potentially valuable resource that could be used in integrated production systems involving small ruminants (Devendra, 1991a). Table 2.1 also gives an indication of the density of animal populations in terms of ruminant livestock units (RLU). The magnitude of this number, in comparison to lower figures for Africa, Latin America and the Near East, emphasizes the imbalance in animal densities between South-East Asia and these other regions.

The limited area of land, and especially arable and permanent crop land, is unlikely to increase in the face of rising animal densities, demand to meet alternative human needs (e.g., industrialisation and housing), increasing urbanisation and growing environmental problems of which salinization is of much concern in South-East Asia. These circumstances suggest that higher agricultural production can only come from increased intensification of arable and cropland, as well as from the area under forests and woodlands.

Farming pattern

Within traditional mixed farming systems, a number of components are involved with varying levels of importance. Rice cultivation (irrigated and rain-fed) is the principal activity, followed by multiple cropping of rice with other annual crops such as groundnuts, soyabean, mungbean and pigeon peas. Perennial cropping is less common given the small size of the farms but coconuts, oil palm and rubber are very common.

Root crops are extensively grown in South-East Asia and include crops like cassava. In addition, vegetables are cultivated in small plots, mainly for home use and sometimes for sale. Animals are of secondary importance but a mixture of species are reared for a variety of reasons (Chapter 3). Fish farming is often carried out simultaneously with rice cultivation but, where ponds are available, more intensive production is common.

EVOLUTION OF SMALL FARM CROP-ANIMAL SYSTEMS

Crop-animal systems have been developed over time. As with other farming systems, the principal determinants of the type of crop and livestock system which has developed at any particular location are the agro-ecological conditions (Duckham and Masefield, 1970; Spedding, 1975; Ruthenberg, 1976). Since livestock systems, especially those involving ruminants, must invariably depend on vegetation or crops for feed, the feed resources provide a direct link between crops and animals. The interaction between the two components and the land, and the resulting effect on productivity, becomes extremely important in the context of the development of such systems.

Figure 2 attempts to provide an illustration of the phases of development in crop-animal systems involving ruminants and is adapted from a classification of world livestock systems by FAO (1980). Climate, and to a lesser extent soil, affects the vegetation that develops and determines whether crops can be grown. These in turn determine the feed base, its quantity, quality and distribution. The feed base, together with the disease challenge, determines the potential animal production systems that may develop. Intermediate phases in the development of both cropping and animal production systems involve shifting agriculture, hunting and herding respectively. Farming system methodology has been especially helpful in the development of integrated crop-animal systems in both irrigated and rain-fed agricultural areas.

Figure 2. Genesis and type of animal production systems in Asia.

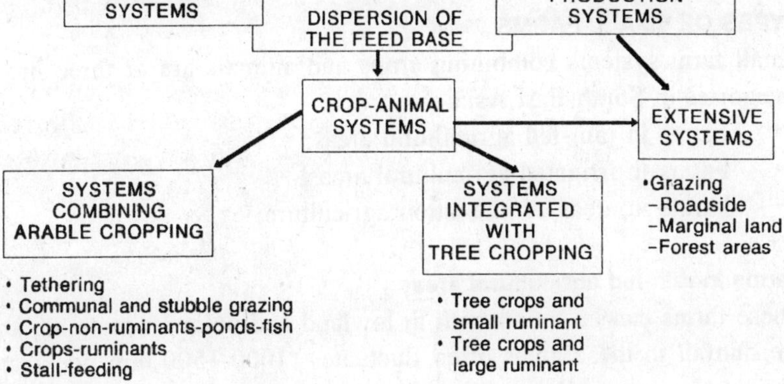

Economic forces, including increases in demand for animal products, prices of alternative feeds and relative prices of outputs, then influence the choice of animal husbandry systems and their integration into what become traditional socio-economic and cultural systems. Growth of incomes and population and the opening up of these systems to outside influences could result in changes which lead to more productive systems or, in cases where the system cannot cope, to decline. Levels of intensification can also shift to commercial-scale production such as in dairying, beef cattle production based on fibrous crop residues or large-scale poultry and duck production for meat and eggs.

In the humid areas of South-East Asia, sedentary systems are possible because feed is generally available in greater abundance and owners of animals are able to stay in one place and graze their stock in the neighbourhood. Crop production is also more important and mixed crop and animal systems can be easily developed. Thus, sedentary systems can be classified into those that are solely or predominantly livestock systems and those that are mixed systems. The basic determinants of this classification are also climate, soils and topography. However, the feed resource base will determine the extent of animal production activities and also the level of intensification.

TYPES OF SMALL FARMS

Small farm systems combining crops and animals are of three broad categories in South-East Asia:

- Farms in rain-fed agricultural areas;
- Farms in irrigated agricultural areas;
- Farms in areas of plantation agriculture.

Farms in rain-fed agricultural areas

These farms can be found both in lowland and upland situations, and the rainfall in these areas often fluctuates (1000-1500 mm per year). The system is usually traditional, sedentary and involves both crops and animals. Both ruminants and non-ruminants are involved but, in general, the upland regions tend to have a higher concentration of small ruminants (goats and sheep), cattle and swamp buffaloes.

The animals are raised for a variety of reasons: food production, draught power, supply of manure and feed, and as a means of capital accumulation. Animals are often sold throughout the year to generate income. Crops and animals are well integrated in these farms and their complementary roles is important for the development of sustainable agriculture in these situations.

Farms in irrigated agricultural areas

The area is usually one of intense crop cultivation: mainly rice, with irrigation. Cereal production is therefore the predominant activity and livestock are secondary to this purpose. Large ruminants, especially swamp buffaloes and cattle, play a vital role here in providing draught power. Small ruminants, although present, are of lesser importance. Pigs, poultry and ducks are also found here; the last of these being especially suited to this environment where they use available feeds and post-harvest losses of rice to great advantage.

In Malaysia, for example, an intensive livestock survey of 5274 farm households in the Muda rice growing area showed that about 87% of all the rural households were engaged in livestock keeping. Of these, 89.4% of all households owned chickens, 47.1% ducks, 26.7% cattle and buffaloes and 7.7% goats. It was also found that individual household owned quite large numbers of poultry and ducks (13-15 birds).

The importance of draught power from cattle and buffaloes on these farms is reflected in Table 2.2 which contains data for farms in the Philippines and Thailand. Of particular significance is the fact that, for farm sizes of up to 2 hectares, both manure and animal power were important. Of the two, animal power was the more important. It is equally interesting to note that only 2.3% of the farms were associated with mechanical power.

Table 2.2 Estimates of farm power sources for different size farms in the Philippines and Thailand (RAPA/FAO, 1989).

Farm size (ha)	Farms with manual power		Farms with animal power		Farms with mechanical power		Farms with mechanical and animal power	
	'000s	%	'000s	%	'000s	%	'000s	%
1	355	40	495	55	19	2	27	3
1-2	263	19	1026	75	23	2	62	4
2-5	267	14	1484	76	40	2	166	8
5	76	7	852	74	31	3	190	16
Total	961	18	3857	72	113	2	445	8

Plate 1. Swamp buffaloes are extremely important in the supply of draught power for cultivating crops and in haulage operations. The photograph illustrates harrowing the paddy field before rice planting in Thailand.

Photo: FAO, Bangkok.

Farms in areas of plantation agriculture

This sector, by its very definition, involves large areas of land under tree crops such as coconuts, oil palm and rubber. However, the countries in this region also have a sizeable proportion of small farms, including government settlement schemes (e.g., Federal Land Development Authority (FELDA) in Malaysia) within which animals are found. The animals are reared mainly for food production: dairy cows for milk, small ruminants for meat and milk production, pigs for meat, and poultry and ducks for meat and egg production.

Types of integrated systems

Integrated crop-livestock production systems involve the combination of one or more types of animal species with crops and fish in a manner such that, although each of these sub-systems may function independently, they are nevertheless complementary and their products additive. The output from one sub-system (e.g., excreta) becomes the input to the other sub-system (e.g., as feed for fish). This synergism and integration of the sub-systems thus produces a greater output than the sum of their individual effects (Edwards, Pullin and Gartner, 1988).

Two broad categories of such systems are identified:

1) Systems combining crops, non-ruminants, ponds and fish. Pigs and ducks are the prevalent animal species found in mainly annual cropping systems. These systems are very important in such countries as China and Vietnam (Figure 3). Important crops that generate feed are sugar cane, cereal crops and multi-purpose trees.
2) Systems combining crops and ruminants. Good examples of such crops include coconuts, oil palms, rubber and fruit trees. The system is potentially important in those regions where tree crops are important such as in South-East Asia.

Figure 3. Integrated pig-fish-duck-vegetable system.

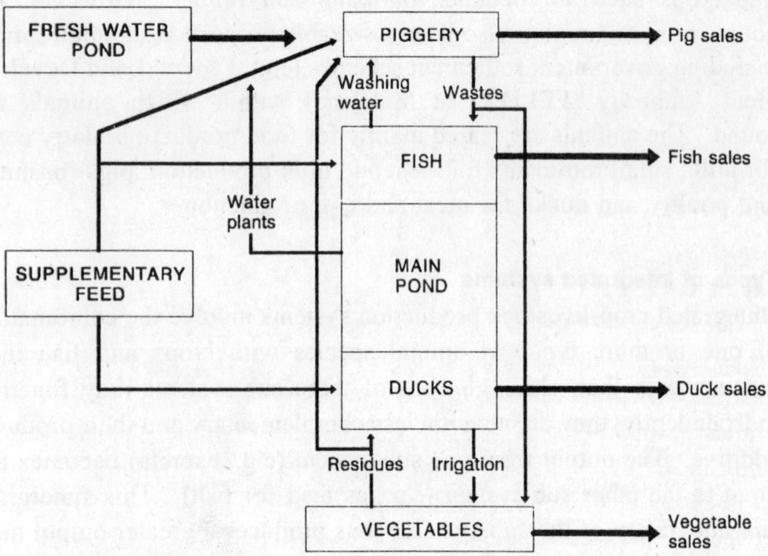

There are eight principal advantages of integrated systems:

- diversification in the use of production resources,
- reduced risk,
- more complete use of farm labour to ensure high farm productivity, income and access to goods and services,
- integration of components which, through their interactions and complementary roles, provides for high efficiency of resource use,
- more efficient use of biological and chemical energy within the system and less dependence on external sources,
- development of sustainable ecological systems that have reduced dependence on external inputs, employ recycling, generate no pollution and are consistent with environmental protection,
- increased economic output, and
- development of stable farm households.

The development of these integrated approaches can promote sustainable agro-forestry systems with complementary advantages of forage production, supply of fuel wood, improvement of soil fertility, maintenance of permanent soil cover and environmental protection. Unfortunately, too much emphasis on commodity-specific research and development in the past has not enabled the development of the types of systems which are potentially sustainable and which are environmentally sound.

CHARACTERISTICS OF SMALL FARMS

Size of holdings

The small size of the holdings is one of the characteristics of small farm systems. The actual size varies between countries. Table 2.3 illustrates differences between countries within the Asian region. The smallest farm sizes occur in Bangladesh, while households cultivating paddy in Sri Lanka have average holdings of 0.3 ha of land.

It is clear that there is considerable variation in the size of holdings between and, in some cases, within countries, depending on the pattern of agriculture. In South-East Asia, the average size of small farms is about 1-2 ha.

Crop-animal systems

Several species of animal usually exist within the mixed farming operations on small farms: buffaloes, cattle, goats, sheep, poultry, pigs, ducks, quails and rabbits, but seldom are all these animals maintained together.

Animals in these mixed crop-animal systems play a multi-purpose role. This ranges from providing food, draught power and capital accumulation to income generation. In these mixed farm situations, animals form an integral part of farming systems. They use the available land and feed materials and are an important focal point for development.

Table 2.3 Variation in the size of small farms in some countries in Asia (Adapted from FAO/UNDP, 1976).

Country	Definition
Bangladesh	a) Subsistence farmers/croppers <0.4 ha.
	b) Viable and potentially viable owners, 0.4 to 0.8 ha.
India	a) Small farmers, 2 to 4 ha of dryland (1 ha wet = 0.8 ha of dryland).
	b) Marginal farmers, 0.8 to 2 ha of dryland and annual income.
	c) Agricultural labourers, <0.8 ha of dryland and annual income.
Indonesia	a) Java 0.66 ha.
	b) Average size was 1.2 ha.
Korea	
Malaysia	a) Less than 1 ha.
	a) Rice farms 1.6 to 1.7 ha.
Nepal	
	b) Rubber smallholdings 2.1 ha.
Philippines	a) Terai, 4 bighas (2.5 ha).
Sri Lanka	
	b) Hills, 1.75 bighas (1.0 ha).
Thailand	a) Average size is 2.8 ha.
	a) Agricultural households, 1.2 ha of land.
	b) Paddy cultivating households, 0.3 ha of land.
	a) Non-canal-irrigated areas: 15 rai*.

* 1 rai = 0.16 ha

The value of animals in this context is also related to their multi-functional use. Buffaloes and cattle are used in small farms to provide draught power, meat and milk and the supply of manure for fuel and to increase soil fertility. Very seldom are they used exclusively for a single purpose, except when specialised dairy breeds like the Holstein-Friesian are used for milk production. In rice growing countries like the Philippines and Thailand, it is not uncommon for farmers to use female swamp buffaloes even in late pregnancy to meet the needs for draught power, e.g. ploughing . Small ruminants (goats and sheep) are also multi-purpose animals, usually valued for meat but also for milk, fibre and skin production, and for manure. Likewise, indigenous pigs and ducks are also used for more than one purpose. Pigs produce meat, manure and lard. Chickens and ducks are used for both meat and egg production.

Low inputs

The low level of inputs is due to a lack of capital and a low risk-oriented outlook. Labour is generally not considered a scarce resource in the small farm situation since unpaid family labour is generally plentiful. The use of one or more animal species in conjunction with crops reduces the vulnerability to economic set-backs. But since the vast majority of small farmers do not have the resources to apply new technology, they continue to remain in the grip of traditional patterns of poverty.

Low level of economic efficiency

Associated with the low input use is an inherent low level of economic efficiency of the total enterprise. It has been estimated that, in the late seventies, about 56% of the agricultural population in Asia had an annual income of 50 US$ per family, barely sustaining life. Both the scale of operation and the technologies applied are not conducive to high economic returns. Thus, the primary strategy and the approach to farming is to make ends meet from diversified agricultural operations which provide a basis for human subsistence.

Diversification of agriculture

Diversification is the backbone of small farm systems. Farmers consciously diversify the use of their resources to produce a mix of activities which are economically rewarding and highly stable. Within a broad variety of agricultural activities, opportunities are created which enable a shifting emphasis, for example between crops and animals, with diversification rather than specialisation being the primary consideration. Thus in Java, goats, sheep, chickens and ducks, are commonly reared in combination with mixed cropping.

The inclusion of animals is based on the consideration that they provide power and food, and are a source of supplementary income, an insurance and a means of investment.

Seldom are more than two species of ruminants reared together. There may be one to two cattle or buffaloes and, more often than not, there are also goats and/or sheep (Devendra, 1982). In the humid tropics where abundant supplies of crop residues are produced from cereal and sugar cane cultivation, the ownership of ruminants provides a means of converting crop residues into useful animal products.

Small farmers

Small farmers and landless labourers have a number of characteristics that are unique to them. These include the following:

- They are essentially poor people who face geographic isolation.
- They continuously experience hunger and rural poverty.
- They have the capacity to adapt and survive hardship.
- They resist changes because of the inability to use new technology.
- Being illiterate, they are not interested in extension materials.
- Women tend to work more hours per day than men and children are often involved in household chores and in the management of small animals.
- They are not commercial producers of specialized livestock products and usually own 1-2 large ruminants, 4-6 small ruminants and/or a few indigenous pigs, poultry and ducks.
- Large ruminants are owned primarily for draught power and secondarily for meat. Animals are reared for multi-purpose use, including the supply of dung and urine.
- They manage their animals as well as feed them from mainly local sources. Farm labour, including women and children, is often used for managing the animals.

- They use meagre farm resources rationally and strive to achieve complementary relationships between the animal and crop components in mixed farm enterprises
- They have secure tenure and can pass on their land and assets to their families and children.

In small farm systems, the farmers provide the bulk of the family labour. The extent of the contribution is dependent on the scale and magnitude of the farm operations. Children are often used for herding small ruminants.

Chapter 3
Animal resources

ANIMAL POPULATIONS

The South-East Asian region has a sizeable population of animals of economic importance. The magnitude of the animal resources is reflected in Table 3.1 which show the high proportion of the world's population of cattle, buffalo, sheep, goats, pigs, ducks and poultry which are found here.

Ruminants (buffaloes, cattle, goats and sheep) are numerically more important than non-ruminants and are generally widely kept. Both categories are important resources for small farmers. They are renewable resources and have varied functions, from food production (meat, milk and eggs) to various miscellaneous benefits such as security, draught power, fertiliser (dung and urine), fuel, utilization of coarse crop residues, social values and recreation (Devendra, 1983).

Over the period 1981-1991, the annual growth rate of specific animal populations varied between 0.3%-9.1%. Among ruminants, the sheep and goat populations grew the fastest (3.6-4.1%), followed by cattle and buffaloes. Among non-ruminants, the chicken population grew at a very rapid rate (9.1%), followed by pigs (2.8%) and ducks (2.6%). Appendix Tables 1-7 provide more details of the animal populations in individual countries between 1981 and 1991. Table 3.1 also provides the projected growth of these populations up to the year 2000.

Within the small ruminant populations, which consistently record high growth rates, the highest was for sheep (4.1%). However, this figure is more a reflection of excessive imports of sheep from Australia and New Zealand to such countries as Malaysia, which has embarked on a massive programme of sheep importation. It has recorded an annual growth rate of 15.1% between 1981-1991, which is over three times the average for South-East Asia. Indonesia recorded a national growth rate of 3.8%. In goats, Thailand has the largest increase of 11.7%, followed by Vietnam and Laos at 10.6% each and Indonesia, 4.0% (Appendix 1, Tables 3 and 4).

Table 3.1 Animal Populations in South-East Asia (FAO, 1991)

Country	Buffaloes ('000s)	Cattle ('000s)	Goats ('000s)	Sheep ('000s)	Poultry (millions)	Ducks ('000s)	Pigs ('000s)	Approx. % ownership in small farms*
Cambodia	760	1560	-	-	7.7	3500	1610	95
Indonesia	3500	10350	11300	5750	590.0	29500	6800	90
Laos	1100	865	143	-	8.0	310	1390	95
Malaysia	190	658	315	200	148.0	5000	2400	70
Myanmar	2080	9310	1040	280	24.0	3566	2250	95
Philippines	2710	1677	2107	30	65.5	8268	8007	80
Thailand	4743	6052	140	178	114.4	17300	5000	76
Vietnam	2929	3282	300	-	81.5	28600	12583	95
TOTAL	18011	34343	15495	6438	1039.1	96044	40039	-
Ave. annual growth rate (%) (1981-1991)	0.3	2.7	3.6	4.1	9.1	2.6	2.8	-
As % of world population	13.2	2.7	3.0	0.6	10.3	17.9	4.8	-
Projected population in 2000	18497	426883	20515	8814	1890.1	118518	501288	-

* These refer mainly to ruminants and ducks. Poultry and pigs in most countries are intensive commercial operations and are found mainly in urban fringe areas.

Plate 2. Typical small farmer's house in Surin, Thailand. Note the housing of cattle under the house.

Photo: C. Chantalakhana

Plate 3. Ducks are very valuable resources throughout South-East Asia and fill an important niche in rice growing areas. The photograph shows ducklings being raised adjacent to rice fields in Vietnam.

These data show that small ruminants are far more important in small farm systems than is normally recognized. The trends in growth are consistent with the expansion of the systems integrating small ruminants and tree crops in the Philippines, Malaysia and Indonesia.

In the case of buffaloes, the overall growth rate is the smallest (0.3%) and countries like Malaysia, the Philippines and Thailand recorded decreases. Indonesia had the largest growth rate of 3.8%, followed by Vietnam (2.4%), Cambodia and Laos (both 2.2%). The growth of the cattle population (2.7%) was much more than that of buffaloes and is also the result of considerable imports of both dairy and beef cattle into the region. The largest increases were noted in Indo-China, with Cambodia (8.6%), Laos and Vietnam (7.5%), followed by Indonesia (3.5%) and Myanmar (0.4%). The Philippines had a negative growth rate.

The annual growth rate is spectacular for poultry and the highest growth rate of between 12.4-12.5% occurred in Indonesia and Malaysia, followed by Cambodia (8.4%) and Vietnam (4.9%). The duck population is growing steadily and the highest growth rate was found in Malaysia (12.4%), followed by Cambodia (8.7%), the Philippines (5.0%), Thailand (2.7%), Vietnam (2.4%) and Indonesia (2.1%). With pigs, very high annual growth rates were noted in Cambodia (16.6%) and Indonesia (8.1%) (Appendix 1, Tables 5-7).

The pig and poultry industries are advanced commercial operations in many countries in South-East Asia. The main reasons for this are the availability and successful transfer of proven technologies in pig and poultry production, support from large private feed mills, the ease of importing feedstuffs, a large and ready market for the products, credit facilities and the rapid turnover of capital investment. The two sectors have already assumed industrial proportions and are usually found in urban-fringe areas which can provide the growing domestic market outlets for the products.

CONTRIBUTION TO GROSS DOMESTIC PRODUCTS (GDP)

Table 3.2 gives an indication of the contribution of animals to agricultural and total Gross Domestic Product (GDP) in some countries in South-East Asia. The livestock share of agricultural GDP was between 6-20%, and livestock share of total GDP was 1.4-5.4%. Unfortunately these figures do not include the contribution of animals to draught power and crop production which would further increase the figures.

Table 3.2 Contribution of animals to agricultural and total gross domestic products (GDP) in some countries in South-East Asia.

Country	Livestock share of agricultural GDP (%)	Livestock share of total GDP (%)
Indonesia	11	2.6
Malaysia	6	1.4
Philippines	20	5.4
Thailand	12	2.0
Average	12.3	2.9

BREEDS

The ruminant resources include a variety of indigenous and introduced animals. In most countries within the Asian region, dairy development is accorded the highest priority in livestock programmes. Indeed, in all countries without exception, dairy development forms the main thrust in animal production. There are several reasons for this, including demand for milk and milk products, means of generating ready income for small farmers, efficiency of protein and energy conversion, entry point to stimulate rural development, means to effectively use family labour, development of cooperatives, improvement in the level of human nutrition and quality of the life of the rural poor, and means of intensifying crop-animal systems in small farms.

Among the dairy breeds, the use of the Holstein-Friesian breed is widespread, followed by the Jersey. A number of important indigenous (*Bos indicus*) cattle breeds exist and include the Kedah-Kelantan in Malaysia, and the Madura and Bali cattle in Indonesia. Among the beef breeds introduced, the Shorthorn, Brahman, Hereford and Charolais are the most common.

Among small ruminants, a variety of exotic sheep breeds have been introduced into the region, mainly from the United Kingdom and Australia. They include the Merino, Dorset Horn, Romney, Wiltshire Horn, Border Leicester, Suffolk and Polled Dorset.

The predominant goat breeds that have been introduced include the Alpine, Saanen, Anglo-Nubian, Toggenburg and German Fawn. Although these various breeds have been introduced and several crossbreeding programmes have been initiated, examples of established crossbreds and proven improved new breeds are very few. One recent achievement was the evolution of two genotypes in Malaysia based on long-term crossbreeding of the indigenous Katjang-type animals with the German Fawn (Mukherjee, 1989). The two crossbreds are the Jermana (50% German Fawn x 50% Katjang) and the Jermasia (75% German Fawn x 25% Katjang).

Among non-ruminants, a number of Chinese breeds have been introduced, including the South China Black, Kwai, Rad, Taoyuan and Kinhwa. These have however been completely overtaken by the introduction of other exotic breeds from industrialised countries like the Large White, Landrace and Duroc for crossbreeding. Several indigenous breeds of poultry and ducks are also found in the small farms; the latter includes the Muscovy.

VALUE OF ANIMALS

In South-East Asia, animals play numerous important functions in small farm systems. They make a variety of contributions (Devendra, 1983; Chantalakhana, 1990) but, for reasons of brevity, these can be grouped into three important functions relating to sustainable development:

- diversification of resources and reduction of socio-economic risks,
- promotion of linkages between systems and resource components (land, water, crops and animals), and
- generation of value-added products (e.g., utilization of fibrous crop residues to produce meat and use of skins).

SIGNIFICANCE OF OWNERSHIP

Animals are seldom raised with a single objective in mind, unlike wool production from sheep in Australia or commercial cattle ranching in Brazil. Rather, the primary reason for rearing animals on small farms is that they serve the material, cultural and recreational needs of the farmers. Thus, rearing animals has the following advantages:

- Income: an important means of earning supplementary income.
- Employment: the creation of employment in animal industries.
- Security: sources of investment, security and stability.
- Power: a source of farm power.
- Food: they provide valuable animal proteins (milk and meat) that are important for nutritional well-being.
- Fertiliser: contribution to farm fertility by the return of dung and urine.
- Fuel: in some countries, buffalo and cattle dung are used as fuel.
- By-product utilization: ruminants enable the economic utilization of non-marketable crop residues.
- Social values: dairy development and ownership of buffaloes have been shown to increase cohesiveness in village activities.
- Recreation: socio-economic impact of animal ownership also includes a recreational contribution to small farmers.

Despite the relatively high ruminant populations and their individual contribution, the development of buffaloes and goats, and to a lesser extent sheep, has been generally neglected. Development strategies have tended to concentrate principally on cattle and the other species warrant much more emphasis in the future in the context of increased efficiency in the use of natural resources.

Plate 4. Intensive small ruminant production is common in several countries. Women play a very important role in the management of goats and sheep in West Java.

The value of animals and especially small ruminants within small farms is also demonstrated by the importance of shared ownership. Attendant advantages of such arrangements are the prevention of overstocking on small land areas and the opportunity they offer to landless and tenant farmers to own animals.

Some idea of the extent of the contribution of small ruminants to total farm income is illustrated by data from highly intensive small farm systems in West Java (Table 3.3). The results indicate that in the lowlands, rubber plantations and upland regions, the percentage contributions to annual income were 17.1, 25.9 and 13.8% respectively. More recently, Devendra (1992a) has reported from an extensive review of the literature that the magnitude of the component contributions from goat rearing was as follows: sale of animals 22.0-25.8%, milk 19.7-76.0% and manure 1.0-4.5% of total farm income.

Table 3.3 Estimated share of total income from small ruminants in West Java (Knipsheer *et al.*, 1983).

Location	No. of farms surveyed	Annual income per farm (IDR)*	Small ruminant income	
			Total (IDR)*	% of annual income
Cerebon (lowland)	79	222000	37593	17.1
Ciburuy (rubber plantations)	66	180000	46671	25.9
Garut (upland)	135	300000	41466	13.8

* In October 1986, 1 US$ = 1625 Indonesian Rupiah (IDR)

ROLE IN ANIMAL-BASED SYSTEMS

There are many examples of integrated farming systems. McDowell and Hildebrand (1980) have identified 10 each for Asia and Africa and 4 for Latin America, in which animals were important. These systems refer to all categories of animal-based enterprises, such as lowland rice and intensive livestock rearing in Asia, pastoral herding in Africa and extensive and intensive livestock production in Latin America.

However, the best examples of integration of animals with mixed cropping systems on small farms are found in the rain-fed areas of South-East Asia. The rain-fed systems are a complex diversity of interactions between animals, crops and the supporting resources. They are characterized by a diversity of animals and crops and a broad spectrum of farming systems.

Table 3.4 is a classification of the prevailing animal-based small farm systems in Asia. For each species, the production objective in relation to type of mixed cropping system is indicated. In the last column of the table, the current importance of the system is assessed in terms of a high, medium or low rating. The rating is based on animal ownership and the table does provide an adequate summary of the current position for the whole of Asia.

The main conclusion that emerges from this table is that, among ruminants, buffaloes and cattle are of high to medium importance, whereas goats and sheep are of medium to low importance. Among non-ruminants, pigs, poultry and ducks are all of medium to low importance in small farm systems.

The role of animals in small farm systems varies from country to country depending on the level of exploitation, the prevailing ecological conditions and whether the animals have to compete with other systems of agricultural production such as tree cropping. In these situations, small ruminants are being more fully integrated with tree cropping systems with the complementary advantages of effective utilization of the available herbage, improvement of soil fertility, maintenance of soil cover and increased total productivity. Large ruminants, on the other hand, utilize the large quantities of crop residues available under lowland situations and are well integrated with mainly annual cropping systems.

RUMINANT PRODUCTION SYSTEMS

The prevailing ruminant production systems in Asia are in three categories:

- Extensive systems.
- Systems combining arable cropping
  - Roadside, communal and arable grazing systems
  - Tethering
  - Cut-and-carry feeding
- Systems integrated with tree cropping.

Taking account of the current patterns of use of the production resources, growing animal populations and available grazing land, it has been suggested that future ruminant production systems in Asia and the Pacific are unlikely to change.

New proposed systems and returns from them would have to be demonstrably superior and changes would need to be supported by major shifts in the availability and use of resources (Mahadevan and Devendra, 1986; Devendra, 1989). This situation is however likely to develop in countries in South-East Asia where land will be increasingly limiting in the face of rising human and animal populations. The principal aim, with good justification, is to make maximum use of the basic feed resources available.

Table 3.4 Animal-based small farm systems in South-East Asia

Species	Production objective	Type of mixed cropping system	Current importance**
I. Ruminants			
Buffaloes	Draught	Rice and field crop cultivation	High
	Beef	Rice cultivation	High
Cattle	Beef	Orchards*, tree crop plantation, rice cultivation	High/medium
	Dairy	Orchards and tree crop plantations	High/medium
	Draught	Rice and field crop cultivation	High
Goats	Meat	Orchards and tree crop plantations	Medium/High
	Milk	Orchards and tree crop plantations	Low
Sheep	Mutton	Orchards and tree crop plantations	Medium/High
II. Non-ruminants			
Pigs	Meat	Intensive vegetable production orchards	Medium/High
Poultry	Meat/eggs	Orchards and intensive vegetable production	Medium/Low
Ducks	Meat/eggs	Orchards, rice cultivation and coastal fishing	Medium/Low

* Includes gardens and unused potentially valuable land.

** Based on ownership by small farmers.

However, more efficient use of the production resources, with the objective of increasing performance per animal, will bring about shifts within the systems through intensification, from the more extensive to systems combining arable cropping and integration with tree cropping systems. The poorest of the resource-poor farmers, and especially the landless, will obviously continue to practise extensive systems but strategies are needed to develop intensive systems that reduce grazing pressure, provide for control of animal numbers and promote sustainability and environmental integrity. Factors which are likely to influence this process in the future include:

- increasing density of animal populations,
- control of grazing ruminants,
- available feed resources,
- growth in human populations and demand for animal products,
- consumer preferences and marketing opportunities, and
- sustainability and environmental integrity.

It is essential to ensure therefore that strategies are designed which are suited and appropriate to small farm systems that are typical of Asian agriculture.

In view of the presence of buffaloes and also very high goat populations with approximately 45 breeds identifiable in Asia, it is appropriate to keep in perspective the considerable differences in feeding behaviour and metabolism of different ruminants and equines. Table 3.5 presents a summary of the main characteristics that are peculiar to individual animal species.

It is equally important to keep in perspective the characteristics and peculiarities of tropical feeds, their extreme variability, utilization, and nutritional constraints that restrict high performance. Many of the tropical feeds are poor quality roughage materials: mainly crop residues whose nutrient content is dominated by cell wall materials. These materials contain sugar rather than starch (e.g., molasses and fruit cake wastes) and the protein content is negligible. Thus, their utilization must take cognisance of the capacity to release dietary energy and nitrogen. In respect of the former, this also necessitates consideration of alternative processing techniques which, for example with alkalis, enables solubilization of the hemicellulose fractions and render increased susceptibility of the cell walls to microbial degradation. Much will depend, of course, on whether the added benefits in terms of animal response is significantly higher than the associated costs of processing and/or treatment (Devendra, 1984; Giaever, 1984; Greenhalgh, 1984).

Table 3.5 Feeding behaviour and metabolism of ruminants and equines (Devendra, 1987).

Species	Arid/Semi-arid zone	Wet zone
Water buffaloes		Grazer (3-5 km/day) Slower rumen movements Use coarse roughages more efficiently Superior N retention
Cattle	Grazer (3-5 km/day) More active Able to walk long distances Dietary N less well digested	Utilizes forages efficiently With coarse roughages, longer retention time in *Bos indicus* cattle
Goats	Browser (8-12 km/day) Bi-pedal stance More active Selective feeding More discerning taste Relishes variety in feeds Utilizes coarse roughages more efficiently Recycling of urea greater	Daily consumption of dry matter up to 6% BW
Sheep	Grazer (3-5 km/day) More sedentary Less discerning taste Recycling of urea less Use coarse roughages less efficiently	Preference is for grass Daily consumption of dry matter up to 3% BW
Camels	Grazer and browser (15-25 km/day) High digestive efficiency for cellulose Less selective Higher efficiency of N utilization Very tolerant to salt Feeding and digestion unimpeded by water restriction	
Asses Horses Mules	Grazer Lower digestive efficiency Digestion mainly in the colon No rumination or eructation Faster rate of passage	

Chapter 4

Contribution to food production

THE CONTRIBUTION OF SMALL FARMS

The contribution made by animals within small farm systems to food production (meat, milk and eggs) is considerable. This contribution is consistent with the relatively large proportions of various animals (70-95% of the individual country populations) found in the small farm sector (Table 3.1).

Table 4.1 summarizes the current contribution of animals to meat, milk and eggs in South-East Asia. Within all categories, there is a steady increase in production. The overall growth rate of total meat production was 3.7%, compared to that for total milk of 4.2% and poultry eggs of 4.8% per annum. Appendix 2, Table 1 provides the details for individual countries.

MEAT PRODUCTION

Of the total meats produced, pig meat accounted for 44.3%, followed by poultry meat (33.0%), beef and veal (11.9%), buffalo meat (5.5%), duck meat (2.9%), goat meat (1.6%) and mutton and lamb (0.8%) (Figure 4).

Among the types of meat produced by ruminants, mutton and lamb had the highest growth rate at 5.6% per annum. However, this is likely to also reflect considerable imports into the region. It was followed by beef and veal (2.9%), goat meat (2.1%) and buffalo meat (2.0%). For beef and veal, the highest production was found in Vietnam (10.1%), followed by Cambodia (4.5%), the Philippines (2.9%) and Laos (2.2%). For buffalo meat, the highest growth rates were recorded by the Philippines (7.5%) and Cambodia (5.9%). Malaysia and Thailand both recorded decreases in buffalo meat production. Thailand had the highest growth rate of mutton and lamb (15.6%), followed by Indonesia (5.9%) and Malaysia (4.9%). High growth rates for goat meat were found in Vietnam (10.2%), Thailand (9.7%), Laos (8.1%) and Philippines (7.0%). Both Indonesia and Malaysia had negative growth rates for goat meat.

Table 4.1 Meat and milk production in South-East Asia ('000 tonnes) 1981-1991 (FAO, 1991)

Category	1981	1985	1991	Annual growth rate (%)
Beef and veal	519.4	569.0	685.5	2.9
Buffalo meat	260.7	280.6	316.6	2.0
Mutton and Lamb	21.6	28.7	46.5	5.6
Goat meat	71.1	77.5	90.6	2.1
Pig meat	1533.0	1864.1	2541.8	5.6
Duck meat	145.9	170.2	165.6	1.4
Poultry	1062.7	1349.4	1895.4	6.2
TOTAL MEAT	2551.7	4339.5	5741.9	3.7
Poultry eggs	164.3	202.5	258.9	4.8
Cow milk	508.1	918.6	1074.6	6.9
Buffalo milk	108.6	123.9	128.3	1.6
Other*	173.6	214.8	254.6	4.1
TOTAL MILK	790.3	1257.3	1457.5	4.2

* Goat and sheep milk

With the exception of duck meat, and in comparison to all meats, poultry and pig meat production grew the fastest. In the case of poultry meat, double figure growth rates were recorded in Malaysia (12.9%), Cambodia (10.4%) and Indonesia (10.3%). High growth rates were also noted in Laos (7.3%), Thailand (7.0%) and Vietnam (4.9%).

Figure 4. Food production from animals in South-East Asia.

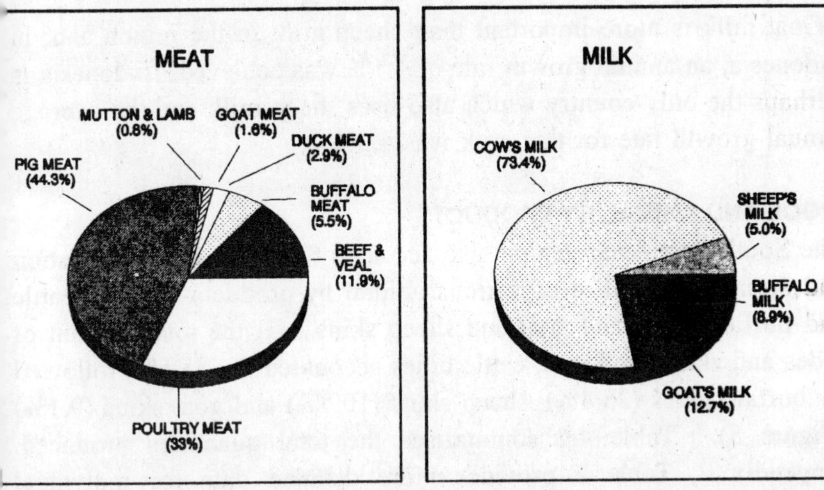

The growth of pig meat production was highest in Cambodia (14.1%), followed by Indonesia (8.4%) and the Philippines (5.5%). Duck meat is emerging as important in a number of countries where relatively high growth rates have been noted. These include the Philippines (10.6%), Laos (6.6%), Cambodia (5.5%) and Indonesia (4.0%).

MILK PRODUCTION

The amount of milk produced in South-East Asia, and especially from small farms, is considerable. This is consistent with the fact that all governments in these countries have given the dairy sector high priority for development, coupled with significant imports of germplasm, dairy production and processing equipment and technology.

Table 4.1 shows that cow milk is the most important among the different types of milk produced and has been growing at the rate of about 6.9% annually. The percentage proportions of milk production are as follows: cow milk (73.4%), goat milk (12.7%), buffalo milk (8.9%) and sheep milk (5.0%) (Figure 4). Among the countries, spectacular annual growth rates for milk production have been recorded in Thailand (24.1%) and Indonesia (13.4%). Lower growth rates have been noted in Laos (4.0%), Vietnam (3.4%) and Myanmar (2.6%).

Goat milk is more important than sheep milk in the region and, in Indonesia, an annual growth rate of 4.1% was achieved. Indonesia is perhaps the only country which also uses sheep milk and the average annual growth rate for this milk was 4.3%.

WOOL AND ANIMAL BY-PRODUCTS

The South-East Asian region also accounts for some wool production and sizeable quantities of various animal by-products, notably cattle and buffalo hides and goat and sheep skins. Of the total amount of hides and skins produced, cattle hides accounted for 55.5%, followed by buffalo hides (25.4%), sheep skins (10.0%) and goat skins (9.1%) (Figure 5). Table 4.2 summarises the total quantities produced. Appendix 2, Table 2 provides more detailed data for individual countries.

Figure 5. Production of animal by-products in South-East Asia.

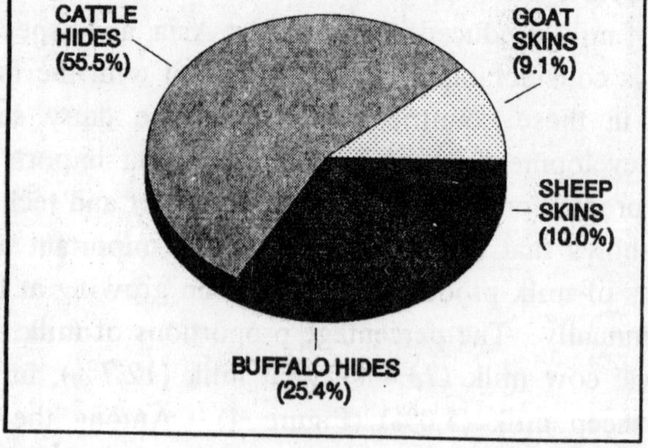

Table 4.2 also shows that, for all categories, there is increasing growth. The wool produced is mostly of the coarse type and is used mainly for carpet production and coarse rugs. Among the animal by-products, production of sheep skins is increasing at the rate of 10.4% and is associated with the increased number of animals being imported into individual countries.

Table 4.2 Production of wool and animal by-products in South-East Asia ('000 tonnes) 1981-1991 (FAO, 1991).

Category	1981	1985	1991	Annual growth rate (%)
Wool, greasy	12.8	15.2	17.8	3.4
Buffalo hides*	41.7	44.9	49.6	1.9
Cattle hides*	89.2	94.8	108.6	2.3
Goat skins*	14.2	15.6	17.9	2.0
Sheep skins*	7.2	11.1	19.6	10.4

* Fresh

CONSUMPTION OF ANIMAL PRODUCTS

Table 4.3 gives an indication of the level of current *per capita* energy and protein supply. Appendix 3, Table 1-7, provides the details of consumption of total meat and that of different animal products for individual countries. Table 4.3 indicates that the highest dietary supply of energy and protein was in Malaysia. The lowest animal protein supply occurred in Indonesia.

Table 4.4 summarises the extent of food consumption of individual animal products, as well as the trends in the growth rates between 1980-1990. Pig and poultry meats were the most highly consumed, followed by buffalo and cattle meats. All other categories of meats consumed recorded annual growth rates of between 6.2-6.5% per year. Milk and egg consumption are also on the increase, with growth rates of 5.7% and 4.2% per year respectively. *Per capita* consumption is also increasing but at a slower rate compared to total consumption.

Table 4.3 ***Per capita* dietary energy and protein supplies in some countries in South-East Asia for the period 1986-1988 (FAO, 1991).**

Country	Energy (Cal)		Protein (g)	
	Total dietary energy	Energy from animal products*	Total dietary protein	Animal Protein
Indonesia	2631	75	57.1	7.8
Malaysia	2665	398	57.8	26.1
Myanmar	2546	122	-	-
Philippines	2235	235	51.5	20.1
Thailand	2288	191	49.1	14.6

* Includes fish and seafood but excludes animal fat.

Table 4.4 **Total food consumption of animal products between 1980-1990 (FAO, 1991)**

Category	Total food consumption (kg/year)		Annual growth rate (%)
	1980	1990	
Buffalo and cattle meat and products	820	1113	3.5
Goat and sheep meat and products	99	129	6.5
Pig meat and products	1363	2488	6.2
Poultry meat and products	1103	1629	6.3
Whole milk	1032	1776	5.7
Eggs and products	768	1131	4.2

As one would expect, considerable differences exist between countries in the pattern of consumption of animal products. Total meat consumption varies from as high as 1181 kg per year in Indonesia to 89 kg per year in Cambodia. In Indonesia, meat from buffaloes and cattle represented a high proportion of the intake as did meat from goats and sheep. Vietnam was the largest consumer of pig meat (888 kg per year), followed by the Philippines (666 kg per year), Thailand (336 kg per year) and Indonesia (305 kg per year). Thailand had the largest consumption of poultry meat (506 kg per year), followed by Malaysia (347 kg per year) and Indonesia (347 kg per year).

Milk consumption was highest in the Philippines (412 kg per year), followed by Myanmar (274 kg per year) and Thailand (256 kg per year), and was lowest in Cambodia (16 kg per year). In egg consumption, Indonesia took the lead with 408 kg per year, followed by the Philippines (317 kg per year) and Thailand (191 kg per year).

DEMAND FOR ANIMAL PRODUCTS

The South-East Asian region is experiencing a relatively high rate of economic growth and this is expected to continue even more vigorously. This economic growth, coupled with increasing pressures of population increase and effects on land use systems, will further increase the demand for food. In this context, there will be a need for increased intensification of existing production systems to meet the demand for food.

The production of meat from non-ruminants (pigs and poultry) will increase faster than that of meat from ruminants (buffaloes, cattle, goats and sheep). This projected increase from pigs and poultry will place considerable demand on energy and protein concentrates to support production, especially coarse grains, cassava, oilseed meals and cakes. Questions will arise about the potential uses of indigenous energy and protein sources like cassava and palm kernel meal compared to the wisdom of exporting these and importing alternatives feeds from elsewhere.

The anticipated economic growth, and therefore peoples' income, is expected to further emphasize the demand for animal products, especially meat, milk and eggs. Sarma and Yeung (1985) have estimated income elasticities of demand for animal products as follows: meat=0.63, milk=0.57 and eggs=1.00. For Asia as a whole, the demand for meat and milk are projected to be the highest among all regions. The demand for milk will be partly met by increasing imports but their extent will be influenced by domestic production as well as by foreign currency restrictions.

Chapter 5
The feed resource base

TYPES OF FEED RESOURCES

The available feed resources can be grouped into four categories: forages, crop residues, agro-industrial by-products (AIBP) and non-conventional feed resources (NCFR). It is appropriate to briefly discuss each of these categories.

Forages

These include grasses (native and introduced) from pastures, non-pasture situations (e.g., fodder belts) and tree leaves from both annual and permanent tree crops. The latter category is usually not considered in pasture and fodder development. In recent years, there has been increasing recognition of their potential value and use by farmers, in view of the variety of tree leaves available for feeding both ruminants and non-ruminants.

Crop residues

Crop residues are mainly fibrous materials that are by-products of crop cultivation. Due to the intensity of and emphasis on crop production in Asia, these form a high percentage of the total volume of feeds produced annually. Notable within this category are the cereal straws on which the majority of the ruminant populations subsist. These cereal straws form the bulk of the fibrous crop residués and, in view of the abundant supply, most research has been directed at this group of feeds.

Crop residues have a low crude protein content, in the range 3.3-13.3% on a dry matter basis. This constitutes a basic limitation to the value of some of the residues (e.g., bagasse and rice straw) which are near the border line of 6-7% dietary crude protein required to promote normal voluntary food intake (VFI). Most of the crop residues are deficient in fermentable energy, reflected by the relatively low organic matter digestibility, and are also low in minerals.

Agro-industrial by-products

The term 'agro-industrial by-products' (AIBP) refers to the by-products derived by the industry from the processing of the main crop and animal products. They are less fibrous in comparison to crop residues, more concentrated and generally have a higher nutrient content. Good examples of AIBP are molasses, rice bran, pineapple waste, palm oil mill effluent (POME) produced from refining palm oil, and coconut cake. In this publication, for reasons of brevity, AIBP is used to include crop residues in general.

Non-conventional feeds

Non-conventional feed resources (NCFR) are identified separately but they form a component of AIBP. The main reason for doing this is to draw special attention to the magnitude and importance of this particular resource base and its economic value. They are currently under-utilized and their is much potential for expanding their use by farmers.

NCFR refers to all those feeds that have not been traditionally used in animal feeding and/or are not normally used in commercially produced rations for animals. Defined in this manner, NCFR embraces a wide diversity of feeds that are typical of and abundant in many countries. Most of the traditional feeds of crop origin tend to originate from annual crops. NCFR, by comparison, includes a variety of feeds from annual, perennial crops and feeds of animal and industrial origin.

It is not easy to draw a distinct demarcation between traditional feeds and NCFR. This is because, in some countries such as Malaysia, what was classified as NCFR may now be subject to increasing emphasis of use. A good example is wheat straw which is very widely used in that country. Palm kernel meal started off as a non-conventional feed but is now being increasingly used by feed millers. Devendra (1992b) has recently published an assessment of non-conventional feed resources in Asia and the Pacific, including strategies for expanding utilization at the small farm level.

QUANTITY AVAILABLE

The approximate amounts of individual feeds actually produced was determined by calculating the amounts produced from cereal production and from other annual and perennial crops. This was achieved by using published information on the land area under the crop, total yield of the crop and the extraction rates applicable to individual crops. The following steps were involved:

1) Estimating the amount of cereal straws that are produced. These include maize stovers, millet, rice, sorghum and wheat straws.
2) Estimating the total amount of AIBP produced from field crops. A total of 11 feeds were identified in this group and included castor bean meal, cassava leaves and waste, cotton seed meal, maize germ meal, rapeseed bran and meal, broken rice and husks, sugar cane bagasse and green tops
3) Quantifying the total amounts of the feeds produced from tree crops. These included cocoa bean waste and pods, coffee by-products, palm press fibre, palm kernel meal, palm oil mill effluent and rubber seed meal.

Table 5.1 presents a summary of the situation. Appendix 4, Tables 1, 2 and 3 present the amounts of cereal straws and AIBP produced from field and tree crops. It is apparent that the total production of cereal straws and AIBP from both field and tree crops accounted for 219 million tonnes in 1989. Of this amount, it is estimated that 32.2% or 70.5 million tonnes are NCFR.

Attention is drawn to the fact that the production of NCFR is very much higher than these figures suggest, as the calculated data do not include the production from a variety of other field crops, statistics for which are not available in the FAO data. Additionally, there are also residues and wastes from animal sources and the processing of food for human consumption which have not been included in the calculations. Finally, there also exist an abundant variety and supply of shrubs and tree fodders that constitute valuable feeds for animals in the region.

Table 5.1 Availability of feedstuffs other than grasses in South-East Asia.

Category	Quantity (million tonnes)*
Cereal straws	145.2
AIBP from field crops	65.6
AIBP from tree crops	8.2
Total	219.0**

* Fresh material

** Of this, approximately 70 million tonnes or 32% is considered to be NCFR.

It is stressed that approximately 80% of the NCFR from field and tree crops are principally suited to feeding ruminants. The utilization of these feeds and other fibrous crop residues by ruminants thus represents a most important function of these animals in South-East Asia. They may, at the present time, be making the most efficient use of these feeds and converting them to useful animal products of value to man.

QUALITATIVE ASPECTS AND NUTRITIVE VALUE

It is not intended to discuss this subject in detail other than to draw attention to the availability of extensive published information in several countries: Thailand (Holm, 1971), the Philippines (Zamora and Baguio, 1984), Malaysia (Devendra, 1979a) and Indonesia (Hartardi *et al.*, 1980). Based on the available data, tables of feed composition applicable to South-East Asia have been published (Harris *et al.*, 1982).

CURRENT METHODS OF UTILIZATION

Current methods of using fibrous crop residues (FCR), together with other feed ingredients, are varied and generally haphazard, in terms of providing a balanced nutrient supply to meet both the energy and protein needs for animal production. This inefficiency has largely contributed to the continuing low productivity of animals in feeding systems and there is considerable scope for improvement.

RUMINANTS

Feeding ruminants in small farm systems is closely linked to the type of production system that is used in individual countries. A comprehensive discussion of these systems is given in the following sections.

Extensive systems

These are usually based on grazing large areas of unproductive or marginal lands which are unable to support crop production. They also include access to more productive tracts of land in locations where land is not limiting and where substantial areas are available for ranching under various land development schemes, such as in north-east Thailand, Mindanao Island in the Philippines and the eastern islands of Indonesia. They cover a thousand or more hectares of land and carry large permanent herds at relatively low stocking rates. The viability of these enterprises has been dependent on a combination of some or all of the following factors:

- availability of surplus stock for purchase at low prices from surrounding smallholders,
- the possibility of improving the genetic base of the stock through crossbreeding,
- ability of the ranch to achieve substantially higher levels of productivity than the smallholders, and
- realization of a premium price for ranch-produced beef.

The total number of animals and people that benefit from the kind of extensive system described above is relatively small. Although output per man is high, the capital investment is also high. The latter includes cost of stock, fences, wells, pumps, handling yards and buildings.

Systems combining arable cropping

Where crop production is important such as in lowland irrigated and rain-fed upland situations, ruminant production systems have evolved so as to ensure that animals contribute to efficient crop production and, at the same time, do not compete for land or cause damage to crops. Thus animals play a supplementary role to arable cropping. Three main types of ruminant production systems that combine with arable cropping are identified. These are:

- Roadside, communal and stubble grazing.
- Tethering.
- Cut-and-carry feeding.

The three are not mutually exclusive. Grazing on roadsides and communal (waste) land may be practised by landless stock owners as well as others when their privately owned lands are under arable crop cultivation. Grazing in rice fields is restricted to periods immediately after harvest when the feeds available consist of the aftermath of the rice crop (*viz.* rice stubble and some regrowth), any weeds which grow in the paddies, the grasses that are found on paddy bunds and browse from shrubs and trees that grow on it. Where multiple cropping is practised, the crop aftermath may be burnt after harvest and stubble grazing may be severely restricted or non-existent.

Tethering is very common throughout South-East Asia and is adopted when there is a need to prevent animals wandering into areas being cropped and also to ensure that they graze down the available feed in a given area before they are moved. This type of confinement feeding is popular in all countries because multiple cropping is very widespread in this region. The animals may be tethered on waste grazing areas close to the farm, on rice fields after harvest to regulate stubble grazing or close to stacks of rice straw to allow self-feeding.

In the cut-and-carry system, a large proportion of the feed is usually brought in from outside the holding because of the small size of holdings in relation to the number of animals kept. The system is subject to the vagaries of seasonal abundance and shortage of forage that are characteristic. Since the livestock are housed most of the time, this results in a growing dependence on increased capital costs of infrastructure and also the use of high priced concentrate feeds, especially during lean periods. As one would expect, the cost of feeding and production in the cut-and-carry system is very much higher than that of grazing, as the results from a study of dairy cattle under simulated small farm conditions showed (Wong *et al*., 1987). On the other hand, land is a major constraint in places like West Java where stall feeding is normal.

Only limited success has been achieved with ruminant production systems that have evolved in association with arable cropping in South-East Asia. This is not surprising when the primary requirement is that all arable land must be used for food crop production and the availability of cultivated forage for animal feeding is limited. Also, the majority of the ruminants (certainly the large ruminants) in this region are maintained mainly for products or services of a non-food nature (e.g., draught power).

Systems integrated with tree cropping

The utilization of available feedstuffs under tree crops, notably coconut, oil palm and rubber, is assuming increasing importance in South-East Asia and also the South Pacific. The advantages of integrating ruminant production with tree crops are as follows:

- Increased fertility of the land via the return of dung urine.
- Control of waste herbage growth.
- Reduced use of herbicides.
- Reduced fertiliser wastage.
- Provision of shade and reduction of heat stress.
- Easier management of the crop.
- Distinct possibilities of increased crop yields and animal products from the land.
- Efficiency of natural resource use and sustainable development.

Plate 5. The integration of small ruminants with tree cropping systems (coconuts, oil palm and rubber) is becoming an increasingly important production system in South-East Asia. The photograph shows sheep integrated with oil palm in Malaysia.

It is of course recognized that the sale of animals and their products do add to the returns from the system but little or no effort has been made to maximise their contribution. In consequence, the stock-carrying capacity of land under tree crops is much more variable than under any other system.

Multi-purpose trees

Associated with integrated systems involving tree crops is the increasing attention being given to the value of multi-purpose trees. The use of these multi-purpose trees in integrated systems with tree crops as fencelines, and especially forage production as feed, promotes the development of sustainable crop-animal systems with complementary advantages of forage production, supply of fuel wood, improved soil fertility, maintenance of soil cover and environmental protection.

There are many advantages of the forages from multi-purpose tree crops (Devendra, 1988) especially in small farms systems:

- Availability in the farms.
- Accessibility.
- Provision of variety in the diet.
- Source of dietary nitrogen, energy, minerals and vitamins.
- Laxative influence on the alimentary system.
- Reduction in the requirements for purchased concentrates.
- Reduced cost of feeding.

Considerable diversity exists in the types of forage supplements of value, particularly to ruminants. The more important ones among these which are widely used in the developing countries are *Acacia* spp., *Ficus* spp., cassava (*Manihot esculenta*), *Erythrina* spp., *Gliricidia* spp., *Leucaena leucocephala*, pigeon pea (*Cajanus cajan*) and *Sesbania* spp.

The potential value of these forages for ruminants has recently been reviewed by Devendra (1990a). The review reached a number of conclusions. Firstly, with all ruminants, the use of various forage supplements consistently increased live weight gain or milk production. Secondly, in many instances, the beneficial response (meat and milk) was associated with a reduced cost of production. Thirdly, of the forage supplements used, the leguminous forages have been particularly advantageous, among which *Leucaena* has been very popular. Fourthly, with only rare exceptions, the stall-feeding or cut-and-carry system was the most common production system used, compared with the grazing situation. Finally, with reference to large ruminants, the research on the value of forage supplements for draught animals is very sparse.

In terms of practical application, a recent review on the inclusion of dietary proteinaceous supplementary forages, especially legumes, and their beneficial effects and practical application suggest the following optimum dietary levels:

- Optimum dietary level on DM basis : 30 - 50%
- As % of live weight : 0.9 - 1.5 %

Plate 6. Forages from multi-purpose trees and other crops are valuable and sustainable feed resources. Cassava (*Manihot esculenta*) leaves is one example and is commonly used in all countries in South-East Asia.

Strategic supplementation

Supplementation of balanced nutrients is undertaken haphazardly for a variety of reasons, chief of which is an inadequate knowledge of the reasons and need for it, potential value of appropriate supplements, notion that energy rather than protein is a more limiting factor and inadequate demonstration of the relevance of and procedures to supply the desired nutrients.

Strategic supplementation is now widely accepted as an important means to increase animal productivity especially on small farms. It is justified because of regular feed shortages that occur, such as during periods of droughts, and the fact that ruminants subsist for most of their life on fibrous crop residues on small farms.

The feeding strategy is thus aimed at the following (Preston and Leng, 1986):

- Create an efficient ecosystem for fermentation digestion of fibre in the rumen.
- Balance the products of fermentative digestion with by-pass nutrients of dietary origin in order to optimise the use of the available energy for productive purposes.

Several alternative strategies have recently been pursued, with the objective of making low quality forages much more useful for production (meat, milk or draught). Foremost in these initiatives are a variety of chemical pre-treatments, of which urea treatment is the most widely used, and the use of multi-nutrient blocks (Leng *et al.*, 1991). The result has been a shift from a sub-maintenance to a maintenance situation, which is achieved by increased intake, increased digestibility or both (Ibrahim *et al.*, 1984), and occasional growth (Perdok *et al.*, 1984; Verma, 1983; Schiere and Wierenga, 1988) and milk production (Davis, 1983) responses.

The use of forage supplements has been secondary to these efforts and is under-estimated. It is however an alternative strategy and, for small farmers who have access to some types of forages, it has enormous potential for application to ruminants (Devendra, 1990a).

NON-RUMINANTS

Feeding non-ruminants (pigs, poultry and ducks) is also a very inefficient process on small farms. The system is generally not intensive and feeding systems are based on available crop residues, AIBP, NCFR and also kitchen remnants. Three broad categories of feeding systems are identifiable:

Scavenging

In this system, the animals (mostly indigenous and unimproved) scavenge on the feeds available particularly in village areas. These include mainly the residues form rice and cash crop cultivation and also kitchen remnants. In general, the productivity of the animals is low and mature weights are reached rather late.

Ducks are integral components of rice farming systems and effectively use both the weeds and remnants of rice harvesting very effectively. In these situations, they are reared extensively in small groups with little supplements. They are raised for a variety of reasons. In central Thailand, for example, ducks are raised by small farmers for meat and eggs, manure production for fish or a combination of these purposes. Typical production data for these species in traditional management systems are as follows:

Pigs - slaughter weights of about 80 kg are reached in 6-7 months.

Poultry - egg production : 120-140 eggs per year;
- mature weight of 1.2-1.5 kg in about 16 weeks.

Ducks - egg production : 160-180 eggs per year;
- mature weight of 1.2-1.5 kg in 8-10 weeks.

Semi-intensive systems

These systems involve some form of confinement with the use of the available feeds on the farm and some concentrates. The system usually applies where the farmer owns a relatively large number of animals and in situations where land is a constraint, in which case some form of confinement feeding is necessary.

With pigs in small farm systems, the Lehmann system of feeding roots such as cassava (*Manihot esculenta*) or sweet potatoes (*Ipomoea batatas*) with limited concentrates is quite common. Forage supplements such as cassava leaves, sweet potato vines, water hyacinth (*Eichhornia crassipes*) and *Ipomoea reptans* are also added. These are often cooked and fed as a slop. Typical slaughter weights of 80 kg are reached in about 24-28 weeks. Where only concentrates are fed, slaughter weights are reached faster but this is unusual because of the rising price of concentrates.

Intensive systems

Intensive systems on small farms are rare because of labour constraints and particularly the preoccupation of the farmer with crop production.

Additionally, inadequate credit and logistical difficulties prevent farmers from purchasing the necessary concentrates.

An increasing trend in many countries in South-East Asia involves home-mixing of feeds using mainly indigenous ingredients. This trend needs to be encouraged to promote the more intensive use of the available feeds and also as a means to increase animal productivity.

CONSTRAINTS TO UTILIZATION

There exist several constraints to efficiency of feed resource use:

- Production is scattered and the quality of feeds is often low. There are also problems of seasonality, processing and storage facilities.
- High cost of handling and collection.
- Non-competitive costs and low product prices.
- Processing is difficult and, in any case, problematical. In tree leaves and leguminous forage supplements, there are some deleterious principles which need to be removed to reduce the effects on animals. Table 5.2 provides a list of toxic principles found in some crop residues, AIBP and tree leaves.
- Lack of managerial and technical skills to utilize the feeds *in situ*.
- Lack of institutional and support services with the participation of farmers.

PRIORITIES FOR FEED RESOURCE USE

Table 5.3 summarises the priorities for using AIBP and NCFR in South-East Asia according to their potential value and importance especially to individual species of animals. It categorises the broad types of feeds, their essential characteristics and the main species which currently utilize them.

It is therefore appropriate to identify potential examples of AIBP which merit particular focus, and which can through interventions, make a significant contribution to improved performance and productivity from the animal resources. Table 5.4 presents a list of some examples of primary feeds appropriate to individual species by location. Both ruminants and non-ruminants are identified. In the former case, mainly meat animals including the use of the swamp buffaloes for draught and meat production are the species of choice.

Irrespective of the choice of feed and location, acceptable and successful feeding systems are those that are simple, practical, within the limits of the farmer's capacity and available resources, and consistently reproducible. The approach at the farm level is to seek optimum rather than maximum performance. Moderate to low levels of animal performance may be biologically inefficient but could be more economically viable than high levels of performance, especially within the limitations of small farm systems. It is equally essential that, in order to ensure the utilization of research results and their impact, there be large scale on-farm testing of the potentially more important feeds involving participation by farmers.

Table 5.2 Examples of toxic principles in some crop residues, agro-industrial by-products and tree fodders.

Type of feed	Toxic principle
Acacia spp.	Cyanogens, oxalate
Banana waste, stems and leaves	Tannins
Cassava leaves, peeling and pomace	HCN 17.5 mg/100 g in leaves)
Castor seed meal	Ricinoleic acid (0.2%)
Cocoa seed husk	Theobromine (Trace)
Coffee seed hulls, pulp	Caffeine and tannins (2.8% DM)
Cottonseed cake	Gossypol (0.05-0.20%)
Cowpea seed meal	Trypsin inhibitor
Kapok	Cycloponopenoid acid
Leucaena leucocephala forage	Mimosine
Palm oil mill effluent	High ash (12-26%)
Rubber seed meal	HCN (9 mg/100 g)
Sesbania sesban forage	Saponins
Water hyacinth	Oxalic acid (2.4% DM)

Table 5.3 Priorities for the utilization of crop residues and agro-industrial by-products (AIBP) by animals in South-East Asia.

Feed source	Characteristics	Species
Energy and protein (eg. rice bran, coconut cake, soyabean meal, poultry litter)	High energy High protein	Pigs, poultry, ducks, lactating ruminants.
Good quality crop residues (eg. cassava leaves)	High protein High energy	Pigs, ducks, lactating ruminants and use as supplements in meat animals.
Medium quality crop residues (eg. sweet potato vines)	Medium protein	Pigs, ruminants (meat and milk).
Low quality crop residues (eg. cereal straws and bagasse)	Low protein Very fibrous	Ruminants (meat and draught).

Notes: 1) The reference to AIBP includes crop residues.
2) Ruminants refer to buffaloes, cattle, goats and sheep

Table 5.4 Some examples of primary feeds for intensive utilization by location.

Type of primary feed	Location	Species
Bananas		
- Waste bananas	Philippines	Beef cattle, ducks
Cassava		
- Leaves	Thailand, Indonesia, Philippines	Beef cattle, goats, and swamp buffaloes
- Pomace	Thailand, Indonesia Philippines	Pigs, ducks, lactating cattle and goats
Maize stover	Philippines, Indonesia	Beef cattle, swamp buffaloes, goats and sheep
Oil palm		
- Palm oil mill effluent	Malaysia	Beef cattle, swamp buffaloes
- Palm press fibre		
- Palm kernel meal		
Rice		
- Bran	Thailand, Indonesia, Philippines	Pigs, poultry and lactating ruminants
- Straw	Thailand, Philippines,	Beef cattle and swamp buffaloes
Sugar cane		
- Tops, bagasse	Thailand, Philippines	Beef cattle and swamp buffaloes

Chapter 6

Major constraints on production

There are a number of major constraints affecting the development of small farm systems. Many of these constraints are inter-related and exert variable limitations on the operational efficiency and, more importantly, the productivity of small farm systems. Since the formulation of development strategies aimed at reducing and/or overcoming these constraints are dependent on an understanding of the issues and the effects, individual constraints are discussed in detail.

SIZE OF SMALL FARMS

The very size of small farms, coupled with a growing problem of land fragmentation, presents considerable problems for their development. The following issues highlight the consequences of this situation:

- Decreased productivity of both crops and animals.
- Shifts in the type of crops grown. In some countries in South-East Asia for example, there has been a switch from rice cultivation to cash crops such as groundnut, cassava or mung-bean. With deterioration of soil fertility, further changes in crop cultivation are also likely.
- Decreased availability of cereal straws as well as other fibrous crop residues.
- Type of animals owned is also likely to be affected by feed constraints. Thus there could also be a shift from large ruminants (swamp buffaloes and cattle) to small ruminants (goats and sheep) and monogastrics (indigenous pigs, poultry and ducks).
- A reduction in the type and number of large ruminants seriously affects the supply of draught power for traction and haulage operations on small farms.

- Since environmental degradation is closely associated with poverty, food security becomes threatened and this often accelerates the use of productive resources by poor households in order to meet their basic needs for survival.
- A combination of environmental degradation and natural resource scarcity adversely affects economic development, stability of rural households and livelihoods of poor people.

These circumstances necessitate both policy, institutional and technical interventions to avoid such deterioration which is contrary to the development challenges of poverty alleviation, increased food production and enhanced livelihood for poor people on small farms. In the absence of such interventions, there is also the distinct possibility that these small farms and small farmers will be relegated to economic isolation.

FAILURE TO CONSIDER THE TOTALITY OF SMALL FARMS

Strategies in the past have mainly been concerned with a vertical, 'top-down' approach which has tended to focus either on crops or on animals as separate commodities, without considering the farm as a whole and the interrelationship of different components (crops, animals, soil and water). Within each of these, disciplinary biases and vested interests have exerted a great influence, often quite inappropriate to the needs of small farms. Thus, in lowland rice-based small farms, there has been concerted promotion of dairy production using Holstein-Friesian crossbreds based on the premise that this enables small farmers to generate quick income, as well as to improve the nutrition of farm households. Whether this type of animal production fits in well and is appropriate in terms of available resources such as suitable feeds, labour supply and management capacity, whether there are assured markets and indeed whether these systems are suited to the needs of the farms and aspirations of farmers is often in doubt. The real need on these small farms may well have been more draught animal power.

It is essential therefore that, in order to promote the development of such farms, their real needs and constraints are clearly identified. The systems approach enables thorough surveys, diagnosis and understanding of the problems and constraints, and permits the development of proposals and technology transfer packages that are appropriate to the needs of these farms, are socially acceptable and likely to have a high adoption rate. Such interventions need to be considered in the context of specific agro-ecosystems in order also to ensure that there will be progress and impact. It is important to stress that the mere development of component technologies *per se* does not constitute a systems approach.

THE SYSTEMS APPROACH

The systems approach is especially relevant and important for the development of small farms in South-East Asia because of their mixed farming nature. It enables a holistic focus on the farm, given the complexity, meagre available resources, need for priorities and complementarity of effort. The following sequential aspects are relevant:

- *Stages*. Description (diagnostic), design, testing and extension.
- *Natural resources*. The diagnostic approach enables an important understanding of the various factors concerned with the meagre availability of resources and the need to ensure appropriate and efficient multiple use within the totality of production, post-production and consumption as a system.
- *Interactions*. Interactions between the different components are inevitable, given the multiple use of the resources and dynamic nature of on-farm research and development, in which there needs to be continued communication between farmers and researchers.
- *Participatory research and development*. There is emphasis on farmers' involvement within the system, utilizing the traditional systems plus productivity-increasing innovations in a progressive way.

- *Eco-regional relevance.* Eco-regional relevance recognizes the specific location and peculiarities, in order to develop appropriate strategies that are technically feasible and socially acceptable to farming communities.
- *Inter-disciplinary approach.* An inter-disciplinary approach is essential to link different sectors: crops, animals, land and water, socio-economics and other appropriate considerations.
- *Monitoring and feedback.* Continuous monitoring enables feedback provided by farming systems research to set priorities for commodity and systems research and definition of strategies for the development of sustainable integrated systems.

EXPERIENCES AND LESSONS LEARNT IN ASIA

It is appropriate to highlight the experiences gained and lessons learnt in farming systems research. This is especially relevant as a good deal of the work done was undertaken in South-East Asia (mainly the Philippines, Thailand and Indonesia), China and also South Asia (mainly Nepal, India, Bangladesh and Pakistan). Zandstra (1991) identifies six major changes:-

- Attention to land use systems has greatly increased.
- Researchers now consider many other factors (e.g., gender effects, stability, institutional support and issues of sustainability) in technology evaluation in addition to the analysis of simple yield differences or even economic benefit.
- Farmer participation has become a reality.
- The enterprise coverage from a predominant focus on crops to broader livestock systems is striking. Cropping systems research is now accompanied by on-farm animal research, rice-fish research and other multi-enterprise approaches
- Process simulation and spatial representations of resources are increasingly used as research and management tools
- Impact analysis is increasing in frequency and, with it, a better understanding of what helps the approach.

On the animal side, considerable progress has been made towards a better understanding of crop-animal systems: their nature, interactions and the effects on both the components involved, as well as the environment, the benefits and effects of using individual animal species in specific situations and their economic benefits. Given the fact that research on crop-animal systems only started about a decade ago, more attention needs to be given to this aspect in considering the totality of small farm systems.

INSTITUTIONAL RIGIDITY AND COMMODITY-FOCUSED RESEARCH

In almost all instances, meeting the needs of small farmers has been frustrated by institutions that are restricted to, and generally only promote, commodity-focused research. In view of the importance of food grains and crops in general, these sectors have received considerable emphasis and the animal component is generally left out of the research programme because it was outside the remit or is the responsibility of some other faculties or divisions. Even where there is recognition of the limitations of such compartmentalisation within institutes or departments, seldom are efforts made to link different sectors so as to address farming systems in their totality.

Such difficulties are often compounded by administrative and professional obstacles and vertical or 'top-down' approaches. These have tended to perpetuate strong commodity-oriented programmes at the expense of developing joint crop-animal research efforts that are well conceived, challenging, and are potentially capable of promoting increased productivity and sustainable development of small farm systems. The systems approach and a production systems focus enables the realization of the latter objectives within a given time frame.

Two commendable examples of institutions which have adopted the systems approach are the Farming Systems Research Institute (FSRI) of Thailand's Department of Agriculture and the Farming Systems and Soil Research Institute (FSSRI) of the University of the Philippines at Los Baños (UPLB). In addition, graduate programs leading to Master of Science in Agricultural Sciences is offered at the Asian Institute of Technology in Bangkok and the University of Chiang Mai in Thailand. A diploma in farming systems research is available at the University of Khon Kaen in Thailand. A farming systems course has also been introduced in the Diploma in Agriculture courses in UPLB.

FORAGE PRODUCTION

Given the growth of the ruminant populations on small farms and projected future trends, there will be a concurrent increased demand for forages (Remenyi and McWilliam, 1986) to feed them, in addition to pressure on other feed resources like crop residues. The following issues are involved:

- Land for increasing forage production and the current intensity of use will be a major limitation on small farms which are already constrained by size.
- Increased forage needs will be partly met by improvements in the quality of available feeds.
- Maximum use will need to be made of all available land, including sloping land, rice bunds and fencelines, for fodder production.
- Periods of fallow need to be reduced in order to increase forage production through more innovative food-feed systems, relay cropping and alley farming.
- Increased forage production through the use of appropriate high yielding varieties, as well as better agronomic management, would be beneficial.
- Multi-purpose trees that can supply fuel and forage and act as a fenceline will also be advantageous. In view of the higher concentration of small ruminant populations in some countries such as Indonesia, attempts to increase fodder production will also need to consider, in particular, the preference of goats for greater variety in the diet

- Increased forage production apart, harvesting and use by animals is largely dependent on available family labour and the high opportunity cost of labour during certain times of the year, e.g., rice harvesting.

ANIMAL BREEDING

The small scale of animal enterprises is a major impediment to the development of sound breeding programmes that are practical and feasible. The small numbers prevent successful implementation of programmes aimed at promoting higher animal productivity.

The only exception to this is dairy development which is sufficiently organised to enable widespread crossbreeding through the use of artificial insemination involving mainly Holstein-Friesian semen. Thus, crossbreeding has produced considerable progress in milk production. However, the problem remains of how to maintain stable populations of the crossbreds produced.

With respect to the other ruminant species like buffaloes, goats and sheep, these animals are bred randomly and often also crossed with exotic breeds in schemes that are generally short-lived and not sustained. Thus with buffaloes, attempts have been made to cross the swamp buffalo (2n = 48 chromosomes), which is valued mainly for draught and meat, with the river buffalo (2n = 50 chromosomes), valued for milk and meat, to produce a triple-purpose animal (draught, milk and meat) but with variable success. In small farm situations, the triple-purpose value of the swamp x river buffalo crossbred is distinctly advantageous. However, inadequate progress has been made in the definition of practical breeding programmes that can sustain stable crossbreds that the small farmer can manage.

Likewise, with goats and sheep, various exotic breeds have been used to cross with the many indigenous animals in South-East Asia. These include the use of a number of European breeds, again with variable success. In general, the use of milch breeds like the Saanen and Alpine goat breeds has not been successful, whereas the use of the dual-purpose Anglo-Nubian breed has been more successful and this is reflected in the existence of such crossbreds in almost all countries.

Sheep breeding is of increasing importance in several countries in the region such as Malaysia and Indonesia, using the Polled Dorset Horn from Australia, the Finish Landrace from New Zealand, and also hair sheep like the Barbados Blackbelly from the Caribbean. It is too early to assess the results of this crossbreeding in practical terms and it will be some years before effective breeding programmes can be defined. Turner (1978) has stressed the importance of undertaking crossbreeding work in the same environment and the need for comparisons under conditions where the crosses will be eventually be used.

One consequence of random, uncontrolled and haphazard breeding in all species is the effect such approaches have on the indigenous genetic populations. It can cause severe erosion and wastage of local breeds and, in the long term, there is the possibility of the loss of valuable genetic material. One example of this is the Katjang goat breed in Indonesia and Malaysia, which is also dispersed throughout many other parts of South-East Asia. The breed is very well known for its hardiness and high fertility but, with excessive crossbreeding and lack of a concerted breeding policy in both Indonesia and Malaysia, numbers of pure bred animals have decreased significantly and it is not known how many still exist. Uncontrolled crossbreeding is also exacerbated by inadequate extension services which have not been effective in preventing such genetic loss.

It is imperative that, if the genetic diversity is to be preserved, there should be more organised breeding policies focused on individual species and specific, individual breeds. Such programmes will also need to consider the need for genetic conservation of the more important breeds in development programmes that can ensure productivity from all the animals on small farms.

The need to match animal genotypes with the environment on small farms needs to consider three approaches:

- *Selection within indigenous breeds.* One important aspect of this approach is that it utilizes the adaptability of indigenous animals. It also gives products that are known and marketable. This method, however, will only give a slow rate of improvement.
- *Importation of breeds for crossing.* This approach can give rapid progress but it is essential to ensure that the crossbred animals are suited to the environment and can be supported by the meagre resources.
- *Importation of improved breeds.* This is not usually a viable approach, especially since small farmers are unable to purchase such breeding stock and maintain it in environments that are often inadequate to support the new breeds. Importation may increase productivity but long term results are likely to be poor.

ANIMAL HEALTH

Animal diseases present a major constraint to animal production in South-East Asia and the extent of the wastage due to disease is very high. This is exacerbated by inadequate funding of veterinary programmes and shortage of veterinary staff, diagnostic and field services, as well as quarantine facilities.

The focus of most governments is to control the incidence of the economically important diseases. These include the following:

- Ruminants: Foot and mouth disease, rinderpest and haemorrhagic septicaemia.
- Pigs: Swine fever and brucellosis.
- Poultry: Newcastle disease.
- Ducks: Duck virus enteritis.

In addition to these, considerable losses also occur through parasitic diseases such as those caused by liver fluke and roundworm (*Toxocara vitullorum*) (RAPA/FAO, 1989). A discussion on the severity of each of these diseases and measures to reduce their effects is beyond the scope of this publication, and attention is drawn to several publications and reports on the subject.

COMMON PROPERTY RIGHTS

Problems of common property rights include several aspects, both social and economic. The central issue is resource management under extensive grazing and in forest areas. Encroachment of cropland on forest areas, for example, is disadvantageous to those who rely upon such areas for grazing and fuel. Improved fodder production schemes which attract only the larger farmers are other examples. Other issues include terms of land titles, inheritance, consolidation, misuse of labour and capital, access to credit, resources and knowledge, and pollution. Women are more disadvantaged in access to credit, resources and knowledge than men.

These aspects are complex and need to be addressed in order to ensure that there is appropriate local level management and community decisions that provide for efficient and non-problematical use of common property resource management.

Equally, there needs to be a better understanding of socio-economic and cultural factors affecting the use of common property resources.

SUPPORT SERVICES

Much of what can be done to increase production at the small farm level is dependent to a very large extent on the extension and support services that are available to small farmers. Firm institutional support is therefore necessary in order to focus not only on the biological variables but also on the supportive elements that are necessary to ensure viability. Extension services tend to be very generalized and very few countries have an extension service that is tailored specifically to meet the demands of small farmers, is sensitive to their requirements and dedicated to the provision of packages of appropriate technology that can have an impact on productivity. Present evidence indicates that animals in general are accorded a low priority in most development programmes.

There is a need for innovative programmes that make greater resources (germplasm, seeds, fertiliser, credit, research and technology) and extension-oriented support services (marketing, training, field programmes and demonstration centres) available to small farmers. Extension of credit facilities, for example, provides a much needed stimulus for a shift from subsistence to economic and sustainable production. Such provisions, deficient in the past, can be substantially increased to stimulate interest in animals within small farm systems. Given the resources and available technology, it is essential to work towards a realistic level of productivity that fits in with prevailing small farm conditions.

MARKET OUTLETS

Inadequate marketing outlets, coupled with the lack of guaranteed prices, is a major deterrent for small farmers and producers. It has often been said that the low productivity of small farms was due to poor management of the resources. While this is so, the main cause however, is the lack of an assured market. Small farmers do have the wisdom and capacity to increase their level of production substantially, if definite marketing outlets are provided.

Successful dairy development in India, for example, is principally attributed to the creation of the cooperative structure and to a price that makes smallholder milk production remunerative. The continuing problem, however, is the fact that the development of small farms does not appear to get the necessary support or assured marketing which is basic to the stimulation of increased production by small farmers (Chantalakhana, 1980).

GROWTH IN ILLITERACY AND ACCELERATED MANPOWER TRAINING

Education, training and extension are fundamental prerequisites for improving the skills and knowledge of the rural population, as well as changing their attitude to new technology. Throughout the developing world, illiteracy presents a major impediment to progress. However, even the most illiterate farmer is responsive to new technology, provided its economic benefits are clearly demonstrated in the prevailing farm situation. Thus training, especially the type that has a practical orientation towards the reality of small farm systems and involves task-oriented teaching and demonstration units, has considerable merit.

Demonstration units can be realistic if they are sited on small farms and involve the farmers themselves, implying consideration for how these farmers feel and then setting objectives that establish confidence by achieving marked production increases without dramatic changes in the system. Associated with this task is the need to establish larger small farmer schemes which involve the participation of several hundred farmers. In this context, it is important to view the education of livestock producers and their advisers who advocate technological change as in integral part of a concerted overall strategy for developing agriculture in general and the livestock industry in particular (Mahadevan, 1984). Additionally, there is also a need for more specific attention at college and university levels to the training of animals scientists and other resource personnel based on a systems approach. This aspect has been largely overlooked in the past.

URBANIZATION

An increasingly alarming problem which concerns many countries in South-East Asia is urbanization. Urbanization involves a shift of people from small farms to cities and urban-fringe areas. The causes of urbanization are many and are linked to poverty, low income, increased hardship and vulnerability. Since this is an increasing trend, a reduction in rural poverty, measured by the percentage of population below the poverty threshold and social indicators, should not be taken as a reduction of overall poverty and could be a reflection of increased urban poverty.

One consequence of this trend is that many small farms are being abandoned because of a combination of inadequate labour supply, aging small farmers and the younger generation pursuing non-agricultural vocations in the cities. The situation is also exacerbated by the rising cost of inputs and inadequate markets for small farmers. This is evident in some parts of Thailand, Malaysia and the Philippines. Good opportunities exist for accelerating appropriate technological interventions and growth, as well as improving the social and economic infrastructure of the rural areas to alleviate the situation.

Chapter 7

Potentially important sustainable technologies

The sustainable use of natural resources to provide for the needs of poor farmers is extremely important where resources are scarce and socio-economic factors are major constraints. It is therefore appropriate to focus on technologies which, with wider application and adoption, are likely to make a major impact on the development and productivity of sustainable small farm systems. Quantum leaps in productivity can only come from the direct application of technologies that involve the utilization of research results, backed by continuing institutional commitment and investment in national R & D programmes which are appropriate to animal production in the region.

ANNUAL CROPPING SYSTEMS

In irrigated lowland cereal cropping and also in rain-fed lowland and upland situations, several new approaches have been attempted which involve both crops and animals in the development of sustainable production systems. These are briefly considered in the following sections.

Food-feed Inter-cropping

Food-feed inter-cropping has two principal advantages. Firstly, the system aims to provide sustainability through the complementary roles of crops and animals. Secondly, appropriate forage crops and crop residues can be made available for feeding both ruminants and non-ruminant animals. Thus the system provides a viable method of providing food for humans and/or cash income, as well as feed for animals. In upland situations, while the food crop is grown during the wet season, forage production from inter-cropping provides feed throughout the dry season.

Plate 7. Food-feed inter-cropping is a potentially important technology in small farm systems. The photograph illustrates the rice-*Desmanthus* system in a rain-fed upland area in the Philippines.

Figure 6. Cropping patterns involving rice and food crop-forage inter-cropping.

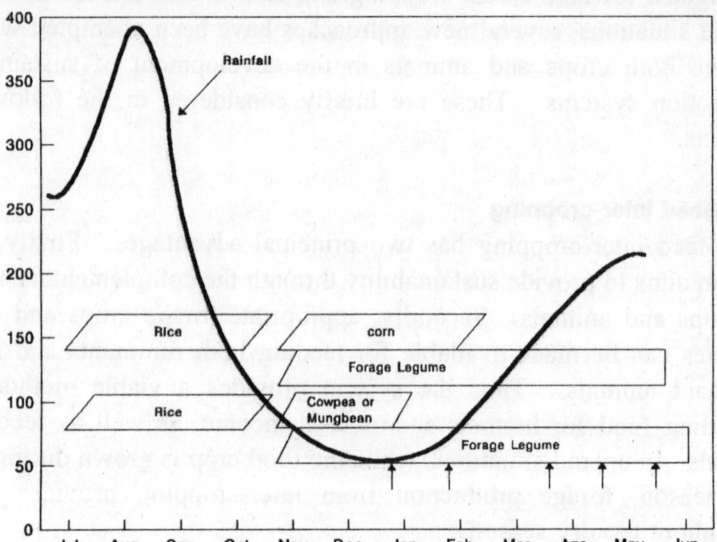

Recently, several attempts have therefore been made in the Philippines and Thailand to develop food-feed systems. Figure 6 shows examples of this practice in the Philippines. Rice is the principal cereal crop but other crops have also been used in the cropping system with the view to increasing the production of animal feeds. Such alternative crops include cowpeas, maize, groundnut, pigeon pea, sorghum and sweet potato. The criteria for the choice of the inter-crop to be used in the system include:

- The type of animals reared.
- Complementarity of food and feed crops.
- Potential forage or crop residue biomass yield.
- Promotion of soil fertility.
- Drought tolerance and extent of the dry season.
- Shade tolerance in upland areas.
- Resource requirements.

Within the concept of food-feed inter-cropping is alley farming, in which rows of leguminous trees are planted between rows of annual crops or semi-perennial crops. The trees provide foliage for the crops, enabling recycling of deep soil nutrients and fixing of atmospheric nitrogen. These nutrients reduce the dependence on chemical fertilisers and enable continuous cropping. The advantages of this system are maintenance and promotion of soil fertility, increase in the supply of animal feeds and fuelwood, and contribution to the development of all year round feeding systems.

The choice and combinations of food and feed crops is important to derive maximum benefits. The following types of crops and intercrops are common in many countries in South-East Asia:

- *Food crops.*

  Cereals: maize, pearl millet, rice, and sorghum.

  Grain legumes: cowpea, groundnut, mungbean and soyabean.

  Root crops: cassava and sweet potatoes.

- *Grasses, forages and feed legumes.*

  Grasses: good drought tolerant examples are buffel grass (*Cenchrus ciliaris*), rhodes grass (*Choris gayana*) and signal grass (*Brachiaria decumbens*).

  Legumes: drought-tolerant examples include *Centrosema macrocarpum*, *Desmanthus viragatus*, stylo (*Stylosanthes guianensis* and *S. scabra*) and siratro (*Macroptilium macrocarpum*).

In rain-fed upland situations in the Philippines, the following intercrop combinations have given promising results (Topark-Ngarm *et al*., 1988):

- Rice + *Desmanthus*
- Maize + *Centrosema*
- Maize + *Desmanthus*
- Sorghum + Siratro
- Sorghum + *Desmanthus*
- Pearl millet + Stylo
- Pearl millet + *Desmanthus*.

The total dry matter yields ranged from 3.28 - 12.93 tonnes/ha during a one year growing period in which the grasses were cut at 60 day intervals at a 30 cm cutting height and the legumes at 50 cm cutting height.

The general tendency is to grow only one crop of rice in both the rain-fed lowland and upland areas where cropping intensity is low. Both areas are important from the standpoint of animal production but, of the two, rain-fed lowland rice areas occupy about 67% of the total land area in Asia, where the bulk of swamp buffaloes, cattle and sheep are found. The drier upland areas generally favour the presence of small ruminants (mainly goats) and large ruminants are also found.

Rice and wheat straw are the main by-products from cereal cultivation and these supply the basic diet for ruminants. They provide bulk and energy for maintenance but not for production. The intakes of these roughage is limited by the low crude protein contents (4-6%) and low digestibility, which necessitates supplementation to meet the requirements for production. Additionally, the reduced feed availability during the dry season, severe weight loss of animals and poor animal performance demand the application of strategies that can ameliorate the situation and make an increased supply of dietary nutrients available to the animal.

Cereal straws (mainly rice and wheat) and other crop residues are the most widely available and cheapest feeds for ruminants. The greatest challenge to their utilization is the development of effective and economic feeding systems for various types of ruminant, based on large amounts of ligno-cellulosic materials. Table 7.1 illustrates the value of integrating two forages: Lablab (*Lablab purpureus*) and *Clitoria ternatea*. The latter is grown after rice for green pods and forage by farmers in the rainfed area of the northern Philippines.

Table 7.1 Grain, residues and forage yields of mungbeans and forage legumes as monocrop and intercrop combinations in the Philippines (T/ha). (Carangal *et al.*, 1988)

Crop combination	Grain	Residues	Forage yield (DM					Total forage & residue
			Initial cut	Regrowth			Total	
				1	2	3		
Mungbean + lablab (cv. Hatiya)	1.02	0.91	1.69	1.98	1.11	0.91	5.59	6.70
Mungbean + lablab (cv. Rongai)	1.00	0.94	1.99	2.43	1.83	1.68	7.93	8.87
Mungbean + *Clitoria*	1.28	1.14	-	1.53	1.16	0.93	3.62	4.76
Mungbean	1.26	1.19	-	-	-	-	-	1.19
Lablab (cv. Hatiya)	-	-	2.70	1.73	1.16	1.40	6.99	6.99
Clitoria	-	-	2.43	2.70	1.06	1.73	8.82	8.82
CV (%)*	18	13	20	32	20	32	10	
LSD**	NS	NS	0.89	1.17	0.49	0.71	1.79	

* Coefficient of variation

** Least significant difference ($P < 0.05$)

No differences were found in grain and residue yields between this and mungbean. The combination of mungbean plus lablab (cv. Rongai) gave the highest forage yield of 7.9 tonnes/ha.

Another type of system which also has potential application and has been shown to be very successful in Africa is alley cropping with both cash crops and multi-purpose trees. This system is also receiving more attention in such countries as the Philippines and Indonesia.

Relay cropping

Relay cropping is an important means to further increase the supply of feeds for farm animals. In relay cropping, a second crop is planted into the first before harvest. Examples of relay cropping are the introduction of legumes (e.g., groundnut and pigeon pea) into the main crop (e.g., rice or wheat). The strategy extends the supply of feeds throughout the year.

Three strata forage system

Dryland farming areas present a variety of problems for crop-animal systems. One major constraint to higher productivity from ruminants is the inadequate availability of good quality feeds especially during the dry season and periods of drought. The development of feeding systems that can increase the supply of good quality forages and dietary nutrients for the animals is therefore especially important to improve the low level of animal performance.

This is shown by the situation in the island of Bali which has approximately three million people and three rainfall zones. Twenty five per cent of the land area is semi-arid with a rainfall of 900-1500 mm/year. Farmers constitute about 70% of the total population and most of them practise mixed crop-animal farming. Among ruminants, Bali cattle are particularly important and in dry parts of the island, income from livestock accounts for about 29-43% of total farm income. Farmers generally own 2-3 cattle which are used as draught animals and for beef production.

Plate 8. The three strata forage system in Bali, involving grasses and ground legumes (1), shrub legumes (2) and fodder trees (3).

Photo: I.M. Nitis.

The feed resources for ruminants in Bali come from native grasses, tree leaves and cereal straws. The dry matter production of these resources is generally very low (approximately 2-2.5 tonnes/year). Dry matter yields can be increased through the introduction of improved grasses as well as forage legumes, e.g., *Leucaena leucocephala* and *Gliricidia sepium*.

Bali cattle are the predominant cattle breed. These generally feed on wayside grasses and crop residues. Live weight gains vary between 100-200 g/day and marketable weights are only reached in about 4-5 years. With improved feeding, as well as concentrate supplementation, it has been shown that daily weight gains of Bali cattle could be increased to between 400-600 g/day and the fattening period could be reduced to less than two years.

These circumstances led to the development and successful demonstration of the Three Strata Forage System, a project supported by the International Development Research Centre (IDRC) of Canada. The system involves grasses and ground legumes (first stratum), shrub legumes (second stratum) and fodder trees (third stratum).

The project ran for 5½ years and several relevant results were found by comparing two types of systems: the Three Strata Forage System (TSFS) and the non-TSFS (NTSFS), with two stocking rates (2 and 4 cattle/ha). The results of the project have been published (Nitis *et al.*, 1990; Lana *et al.*, 1990; Arga, 1990 and Nuraini, 1990). Table 7.2 presents some of the results and the following summarizes the main highlights:

- The allocation of 0.09 ha of land as a forage boundary within the TSFS produced 98% more forage than the 0.25 ha of natural pasture. With the additional 2000 shrubs and 42 trees, the total wet and dry season forage production in the TSFS was 91% more than that of NTSFS.
- *Stylosanthes*, *Centrosema*, *Acacia*, *Gliricidia* and *Leucaena* provided increased dietary nutrients in the TSFS. Consequently, cattle raised in the TSFS gained 19% more live weight and reached market weight 13% faster. Additionally, the carcasses of these animals had generally more fat.
- The availability of increased forages also enabled higher stocking rates and live weights per hectare to be achieved: 3.2 animal units (375 kg) /ha/year in the TSFS compared to 2.1 animal units (122 kg) /ha/year.
- Cattle in the TSFS were less affected by endoparasites. This was presumably due to less contact with the traditional cattle, since the TSFS cattle were always kept in confinement.
- The introduction of forage legumes into the TSFS reduced soil erosion by as much as 57% in the TSFS compared to the NTSFS. Additionally, the fertility of the soil in the TSFS was also considerably improved.

- With the presence of 2000 shrubs and 42 trees lopped twice a year, the firewood production of 0.25 ha TSFS was 1.5 tonnes per year. Since the firewood requirement of a household was 4.2 tonnes *per annum*, the TSFS supplied 64% of the farmer's requirement.

Farmers in the TSFS spent less time managing their cattle and also had more access to increased supplies of firewood in the TSFS compared to the NTSFS. More importantly, these same farmers benefitted by an increase of 31% (IDR 120,631) in income compared to the NTSFS.

Further research and development, with the objective of creating a more sustainable TSFS, involves the introduction of goats into the system. The justifications for this are twofold: the provincial government of Bali is officially promoting their value, especially in dryland farming areas, and potential possibilities exist for generating increased additional income. Goats will also provide greater flexibility of resource use by farmers. On a live weight basis, one Bali bull weighing 375 kg is equivalent to 6 goats of 30 kg live weight each. When feed is limited during the dry season, it is easier to reduce the number of goats than that of cattle. A theoretical calculation suggests that, with shrubs and tree fodders, increased carrying capacity is feasible. The continuing efforts will also involve detailed studies on the utilization of *Gliricidia* forage.

Crop-animal systems in lowland rain-fed areas

The value of crop-animal systems lies in their positive contribution to sustainability and economic growth. The economic impact can be considerable and is reflected in the results of work done over 6 years (1985-1990) in difficult transmigration farming system sites in Sumatra, Indonesia. Each farming family was allocated 5 ha of land (1.5 ha for food crops, 1 ha reserve for food crops, 1 ha for rubber, 0.25 ha for grass and 0.25 ha home lot) within the settlement.

Table 7.2 Comparative productivity of three strata and non-three strata forage systems (kg dry weight per plot per year) (Nitis *et al.*, 1990).

Parameter	TSFS*	NTSFS**
Food	853	1268
Straw	750	1218
First stratum	455	-
Second stratum	310	-
Third stratum	15	-
Shrubs	-	132
Trees	-	2
Improved grasses	-	10
Native grasses	-	242
Firewood	1049	475
Cattle live weight gain (kg/3 years)	186	166
Carrying capacity (cattle/ha)	4	2
Maximum live weight (kg/head)	300	200
Soil erosion (mm/2 years)	11	20

* Three strata forage system
** Non-three strata forage system.

The main objective of the research and development effort is to assess the value and contribution of four models aimed at achieving sustainable farming systems and stability of transmigrants. A central goal was to generate a minimum target income of US$ 1500/family/year. The models tested were:

(A) Farmers' existing system without animals.
(B) Farmers' existing system with animals.
(C) Introduced farming system with animals (1 cow + 3 goats + 11 chickens).

(D) Introduced farming system with animals (2 cows + 5 goats + 23 chickens).

The results indicated that Model C was the most promising and was able to generate the minimum target income. Over the 6-year study period, the increased net income compared to Model A was Rp 900,000/ha/year, equivalent to US$ 458/ha/year. Of this, the contribution by rubber, food crops and animals were 53, 30 and 17 % respectively (Table 7.3)

Table 7.3 Economic impact of crop-animal systems in transmigration schemes Batumarta, Sumatra, Indonesia (CRIC, 1991)

Farming system*	US$/ha/year**	Contribution to income (%)	
Model A	1230	Rubber -	53%
Model C	2055	Food crops -	30%
Net gain	825	Animals -	17%

* Model (A) - Farmer's existing system without animals
Model (C) - Introduced farming system with animals (1 cow + 3 goats + 11 chickens)

** 1 US$ = 1963 In. Rups (approx.)

INTEGRATED ANIMAL-FISH-CROPS SYSTEMS

A variety of integrated systems are prevalent throughout Asia involving one or more animals. These are of two broad categories (Devendra, 1991a):

Systems combining crops, non-ruminants, ponds and fish

These systems directly involve the use of fish, mainly non-ruminants like pigs and ducks and also crop production such as vegetables and rice. The systems are more prevalent in annual cropping systems.

A sustainable system which is widely practised in South-East Asia and China involves pig production integrated with fish farming, duck keeping and vegetable production, or a combination of these (Devendra and Fuller, 1979). The inter-relationships between the component parts of the system was illustrated in Figure 3. The system is based on the use of ponds which not only meets the needs of pigs, but also enables fish and ducks to be reared. Water is also useful for vegetables production.

The main advantages of the system are:

- Efficiency of scarce resource use in small farms.
- Reduced dependence on purchased concentrates for pigs, ducks and fish.
- Reduced cost of production.
- Bioenergetic efficiency.
- Reduced pollution.
- Increased self-reliance.
- Sustainability.

Systems combining crops and ruminants

These are essentially terrestrial and are concerned mainly with perennial crops and ruminants (buffaloes, cattle, goats and sheep) in systems that do not involve ponds. This is described under the section on tree cropping systems.

TREE CROPPING SYSTEMS

Integrating ruminants with tree crops such as coconuts, oil palm and rubber constitutes an important production system but it has not been adequately explored in South-East Asia and the Pacific. Systems integrated with tree cropping are especially common in the humid and sub-humid regions where there is intensive crop production. Although the system is not new, the process of integration with tree crops to ensure more sustainable land use has not been given adequate research and development attention. The advantages of the system have already been indicated (Chapter 5).

The importance of integrating small ruminants with tree crops such as coconuts, oil palm and rubber also involves the use of multi-purpose trees such as *Leucaena leucocephala*, *Acacia* spp., *Gliricidia* spp. and

Prosopis spp. Agro-forestry systems have the complementary advantages of forage production, supply of fuelwood and domestic tree products, improvement of soil fertility and maintenance of permanent soil cover, which together are coupled to efficient use of the natural resources and environmental protection. Additionally, combined cultivation of such trees and forests also promotes integrated watershed management, especially in semi-arid and arid areas where water is critical for upland catchment situations.

A specific example of the economic benefits of integrating ruminants with tree crops concerns the case study on an oil palm estate that allocated a portion of the grazing land within the estate to the workers for grazing their animals. For the first two years (1980 and 1981), only cattle were owned and grazed; in 1982 and 1983 however, goats were also introduced in addition to cattle. This was done because of their economic importance and capacity to supply both meat and milk in the estate.

The comparison of the grazed and non-grazed area involving both young and mature trees is valid in that it involved both the same area of 71-135 ha and, more particularly, the fact that both areas were on the same type of soil type. The improvement in yield due to the effect of grazing cattle and goats over the four years was 2.15-5.16 tonnes of fresh fruit bunches per hectare per year (Table 7.4). When translated into the total area available for grazing and adding the sale value per tonne of fresh fruit yield, the economic advantage is substantial. The result in economic terms is similar to the findings in West Java of integrating goats and sheep under rubber. The presence of legumes is of definite advantage and it has been calculated that the amount of nitrogen utilized by the animal and excreted in the faeces and urine increases with the presence of the legume cover.

More recently, a study has been reported on the integration of goats with pine (*Pinus insularis*) in the Philippines. A stocking rate of four goats/ha did not cause significant soil loss nor reduction in soil bulk density, compaction and infiltration rates. Thinning or reducing the crown density of the pine stand increased tree growth as well as forage production. The daily weight gains were impressive and averaged 99 to 129 g/day/goat. The integration demonstrated an ecological and economically viable farming practice for the forest dwellers which is sustainable (Penafiel and Veracion, 1987).

Table 7.4 The effect of mixed cattle and goat grazing on the yield of fresh fruits in oil palm cultivation in Malaysia (Devendra, 1991b).

Year	Grazed area	Non-grazed area	Difference
	Fresh fruit bunches (Tonnes per ha per year)		
1980	30.55 (C)*	25.61	4.94
1981	17.69 (C)	15.87	1.82
1982	25.12 (C&G)	22.97	2.15
1983	23.45 (C&G)	18.29	5.16
Mean	24.45	20.69	3.52

* C = cattle
C & G = cattle and goats

PRACTICAL BENEFITS OF SUPPLEMENTATION

Two innovative approaches that combine the new concepts in feeding and nutrition of animals and which provide a more balanced supply of nutrients concern firstly the use of multi-nutrient blocks licks and secondly leguminous forages as strategic supplements for ruminants.

Multi-nutrient block licks are now being increasingly used in many parts of Asia by small farmers to correct the imbalanced nutrient supply in feeding systems for ruminants. These blocks primarily provide for the needs of an efficient rumen ecosystem: a source of fermentable nitrogen, minerals and vitamins, amino acids and peptides. The response have been very favourable in terms of economic benefit and increased milk production which is normally achieved by concentrate supplementation. In India, backed by official support, this has led to more widespread development and use of the blocks in the village situation.

In recent years, there has been considerable progress in the use of multi-nutrient block licks as an innovative system of providing supplements to ruminants subsisting mainly on coarse roughage such as cereal straws. These block licks have several advantages:

- Provision of nutrients (fermentable nitrogen, minerals and vitamins).
- Administration of chemicals to manipulate rumen fermentation (e.g., methane inhibitors)
- Administration of drugs
- Administration of hormones (eg. for manipulating growth)
- Administration of chemicals to control fly development in faeces, which could be important for human health.

An example of large scale acceptance of a specific technology, which demonstrates how feed composition properly integrated with nutritional knowledge can have an impact, is the on-farm utilization of multi-nutrient blocks based on urea-molasses in India. Under village conditions, providing cattle and buffaloes with blocks has led to a substantial increase in milk yield and milk fat percentage (Table 7.5). When these blocks were introduced into the traditional system, the average increase in milk yield of buffaloes and cows was about 0.5 l/day, indicating that these block licks corrected a widespread deficiency of nutrients in diets normally fed to cattle and buffaloes in village situations and proved cost-effective.

Supplementation with leguminous forages is very promising and *Gliricidia sepium* and *Erythrina* offer considerable potential. They provide valuable rumen fermentable nitrogen and by-pass proteins to diets based on fibrous crop residues. Since such forages are grown by small farmers, their more intensive use is an important strategy to reduce the cost of feeding and dependence on concentrates for dairy animals, as well as to promote increased productivity. The potential benefits of using a variety of leguminous forages and the beneficial responses in buffaloes, cattle, goats and sheep has been reported (Devendra, 1990a).

Table 7.5 Average milk and milk fat sold per buffalo before and after the introduction of molasses/urea blocks into villages in the Kaira Milk Producing Union Ltd., Anand, India (Kunju, 1986)

Village	Average milk sold (kg/animal/day)		Fat (g/day)	
	Before (no block)	With Block	Before (no block)	With block
Alwa	4.8	5.9	330	450
Punadhara	4.0	4.8	270	340
Fulgenamuwada	2.4	3.5	160	280
Hirapura	4.2	5.2	350	480
Banroli	3.6	4.2	270	380
Dehgam	4.3	4.7	310	350

PROCESSING AND CHOPPING

Processing (chopping and grinding) of some crop residues may be feasible in some small farm situations and, associated with this, is the development of complete feeds. However, this will be largely dependent on the availability of feeds such as rice straw, cassava roots or leucaena forage, type and number of animals to be fed and extent of intensification. An overriding consideration that will determine the value of these approaches is the demonstration of economic benefits. For successful application and acceptance at the farm level however, practical technologies need to be simple, within the limits of the farmers' capacity and resource availability, convincing and consistently reproducible.

ALL YEAR ROUND FEEDING SYSTEMS

The strategy to increase feeds within small farm systems should have the final objective of developing all year round feeding systems appropriate to the prevailing situations. This objective has to be identified with sustainability in order to ensure efficient use of both animals and crops in integrated systems. In this quest, maximizing feed production is essential and the following approaches are feasible:

- Integrating with cereal crops.
- Relay cropping.
- Food-feed cropping systems.
- Intensive use of available crop residues.
- Forage production on rice bunds.
- Alley cropping.
- Three-strata forage system in dryland areas.

The two key elements in the use of one or more of these approaches are quantification of the feeds produced throughout the year and efficiency of utilization of the feedstuffs by the available animals. The former enables in turn, the determination of feed balance sheets, the extent to which animals can be supported and associated with feed supplies and the critical periods during which feed deficits need to be corrected to ensure that animals production is not impede but can be sustained.

The scope for increasing the efficiency of feed utilization is enormous. More innovative feeding systems are necessary that can sustain all year round feeding in more intensive systems of production. These include various pre-treatments, supplementation and also the use of multi-nutrient block licks.

UTILIZATION OF RESEARCH RESULTS AT THE SMALL FARM LEVEL

The utilization of such research results in Asia and the Pacific merits the highest priority because feeds and feeding represent the main constraint to animal production. The bulk of the work done in this discipline has been mainly concerned with screening and evaluation at the research station level, with only limited attention to development. This is borne out by a review of the ,proceedings of national and regional meetings on the subject.

There have been a total of 31 regional meetings in Asia, over the period 1977-1991 equivalent to about two meetings annually. The results and information presented in all these meetings are generally sound and have significantly contributed to increased fundamental knowledge. Yet, the results of research have not made any discernable impact on the more intensive and expanded utilization of the available feeds or the productivity of farm animals. This observation is reflected further in the conclusion on a review of research on the utilization of rice straw (Doyle, Devendra and Pearce, 1986). The authors concluded that the importance of evaluating new technologies through on-farm testing and demonstration far out-weighed the need for further documentation of the effects of supplementation or pre-treatments.

Phases in on-farm research

The question can then be asked: how can the utilization of research results on cereal straws be accelerated and applied to the farm level? Associated with this: why has there been poor rate of adoption of the available technologies? On-farm animal research (OFAR) is a way to extend the adoption of technology packages that are likely to be acceptable both economically and socially to the farmers, taking into account all the interacting components unique to farming systems and specific ecosystems. It is a means of identifying and addressing the constraints on the adoption of new feeding systems and the extent to which these can contribute to sustainability (Devendra, 1990b). Two phases are involved:

Phase I: Information needed by farmers and their advisers

1. Choice of feeds and their availability over seasons.
2. Detailed information on composition of feeds, nutritional value, prediction of changes during periods of production, capacity to meet production targets and capability of filling any nutritional gap.
3. Effects of strategic supplementation on animal performance, economic response, sustained production of the basal feed resources and methodology of use.
4. Appropriate feeding systems.

5. Level and type of production (meat, milk and/or draught).
6. Realistic production targets.

Phase II: Mechanisms for the delivery of information to farmers

7. Methodology: balance between fundamental and applied research.
8. Linkages across disciplines and institutions.
9. Demonstration of economic benefit.
10. Large scale on-farm testing.
11. *In situ* utilization.
12. Farmer participation.
13. Definition of a model for feeding resource development.

Intensification of feed resource use is implicit and, with it, a shift from more extensive systems to semi-intensive and intensive systems. Presently, small farmers, agricultural labourers and agricultural tenants raise ruminants mainly in extensive grazing systems. The poorest of these resource-poor farmers, and especially the landless, will obviously continue practising the system but the long term sustainability of such grazing systems is questionable. The strategy to promote semi-intensive and intensive feeding systems would reduce prevailing grazing pressures. The more progressive of the poor farmers are willing to adopt improved systems which can provide greater control of animals and higher incomes, provided the benefits can be demonstrated by on-farm testing of sustainable production systems.

Criteria for development orientation

Increased and more concerted development to promote the better utilization of feedstuffs by farm animals also requires attention to several important criteria affecting on-farm activities. These include:

- Objectives of production
- The treatments involved.
- The precise methodologies to support the work.
- The measurements to be undertaken.

- Type and value of the inputs used and the outputs derived from on-farm testing.
- Extent of farmer participation and consideration of gender issues.
- Economic analysis of the results.
- Marketing.

The strategy for large-scale testing needs to consider project formulation and relevance of the research from inception and basic research, through to on-farm work involving the participation of farmer and subsequent development. The benefits of coordinated programmes are likely to be: more efficient resource use, increased animal performance, cost effectiveness, increased farm incomes, reduced pollution and maintenance of environmental integrity. Unfortunately, few such development-oriented programmes exist or have been attempted and much more can be done to formulate such activities in the Asian region.

The protocols for such efforts need to be adequately examined. Carefully designed programmes and increased on-farm testing are priorities. The on-farm tests need to be simple, practical, appropriate to the farmers' resources and need to be conducted jointly by participating farmers who are receptive to change and the benefits of new technology. At present, there are few such programmes concerned with feed utilization.

The final objective is to link the work to the development of all-year-round feeding systems. Such systems enable a definition of what types of feedstuffs can be used at different times of the year, including necessary interventions to overcome critical periods of feed shortages.

Large scale on-farm testing

Beyond the demonstration of the economic benefits of new feeding systems at the station level, the next step is to implement large-scale application of the results on-farm. Community-based participation is essential and such work should also address important gender issues.

Wider adoption of new technologies can be achieved through the on-farm application of complete systems and the development of sustainable crop-animal components that addresses the totality of production, post-production and consumption systems. Figure 7 identifies the potential technologies and the components of whole farm production to consumption systems.

Figure 7. Whole farm production and consumption systems.

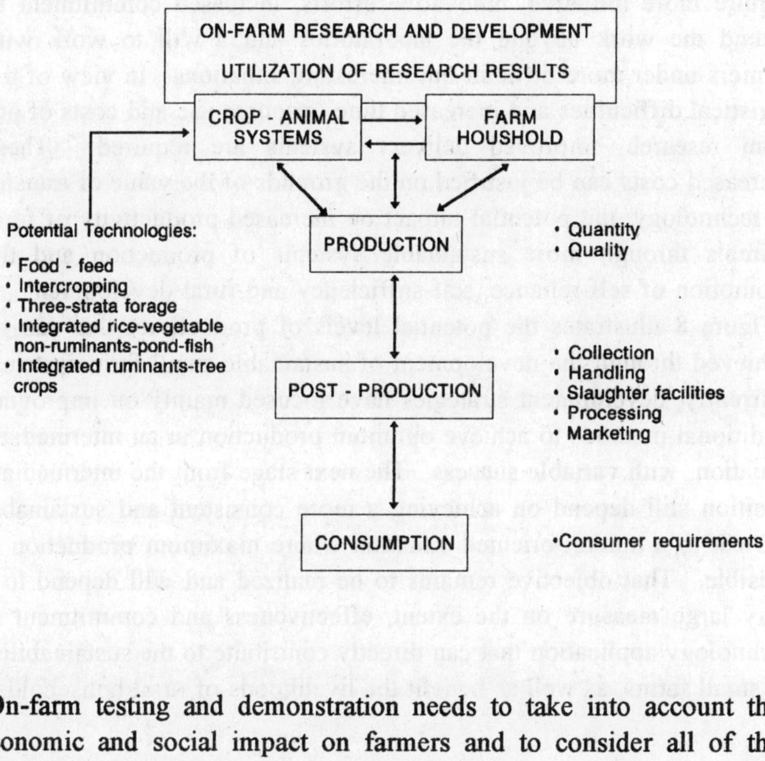

On-farm testing and demonstration needs to take into account the economic and social impact on farmers and to consider all of the interacting components unique to small farm systems. This is a means of addressing constraints to the adoption of new technologies and, in many countries, the importance of such trials merits the highest priority in comparison to further documentation of the effects of supplementation or pre-treatments. Appropriate methods for conducting on-farm research, procedures and economic analysis have recently been reported (Amir and Knipscheer, 1989).

Presently, there is an imbalance in the proportion of research programmes undertaken at the station level compared to on-farm participatory research with farmers. A major shift is required towards a farm-based approach. This calls for a move away from the more fundamentally-oriented research at the station or university farm level, to increased application in real farm situations. These efforts will require more initiative, innovative efforts, increased commitment to extend the work beyond the laboratories and a will to work with farmers under more difficult but interesting situations. In view of the logistical difficulties and increased time, resource use and costs of on-farm research, improved delivery systems are required. These increased costs can be justified on the grounds of the value of transfer of technology, the potential impact on increased productivity of farm animals through more sustainable systems of production and the promotion of self-reliance, self-sufficiency and rural development.

Figure 8 illustrates the potential levels of productivity that can be achieved through the development of sustainable small farm systems. Currently, development strategies have focused mainly on improving traditional methods to achieve optimum production in an intermediate situation, with variable success. The next stage from the intermediate position still depend on achieving a more consistent and sustainable growth to a market-oriented situation where maximum production is feasible. That objective remains to be realized and will depend to a very large measure on the extent, effectiveness and commitment to technology application that can directly contribute to the sustainability of small farms, as well as benefit the livelihoods of rural households.

Figure 8. Potential levels of productivity from traditional market-oriented systems and the development of sustainable small farms.

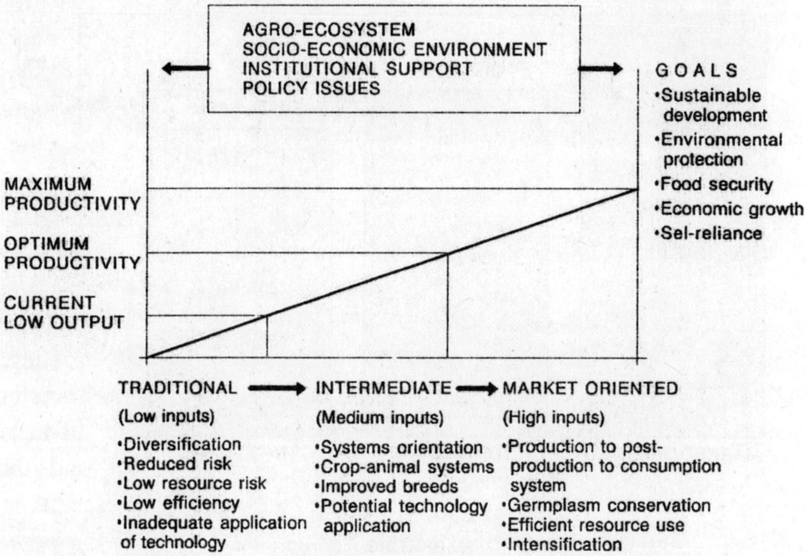

Figure 9 provides one example of the magnitude of differences that could be achieved in the total meat yield of goats (adapted from Devendra, 1979b). The potential yield differences are 12.8% and 36.8% in the intermediate and market-oriented levels. The factors contributing to these in terms of orders of magnitude are feeding and nutrition 40%, technology application 30%, reduced disease 20%, adaptation 10% and marketing 5%. Potential improvements through improved feeding and nutrition have also been demonstrated in sheep (Soetanto, 1986) and buffaloes (Putu *et al.*, 1983) in Indonesia and cattle in Malaysia (Devendra and Lee, 1975).

Figure 9. The magnitude of the differences in total edible meat yields of goats and factors contributing to them.

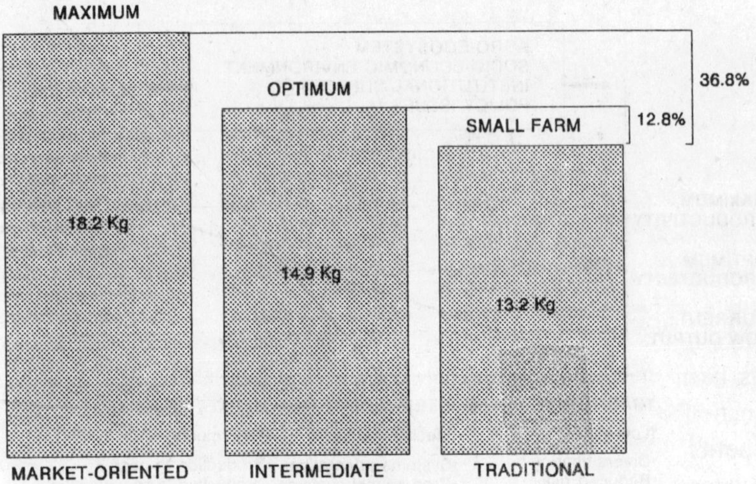

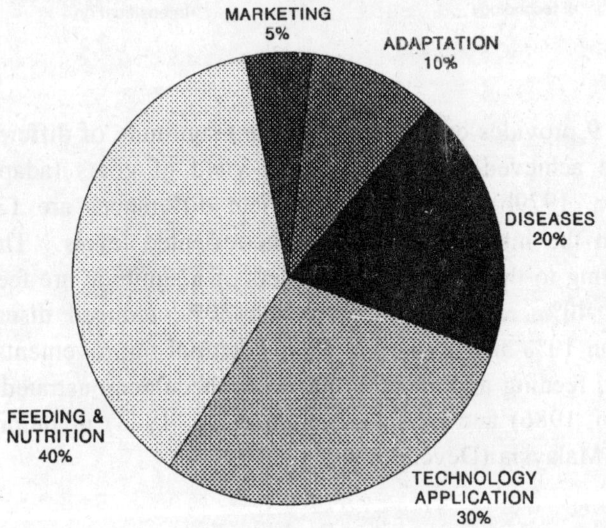

Chapter 8

The development of integrated systems

Although integrated farming systems have long been practised and are widespread in South-East Asia, their importance and potential contribution to sustainable development has been inadequately appreciated. Also, there are few systems that have been able to consistently demonstrate sustainable production and economic benefits. There are several reasons for this, among which is the fact that there has been very little research aimed at understanding the nature and functions of the systems or measuring their productivity and economic benefits. This is reflected in poor documentation of the value of these systems and their development. Another reason is associated with the notion of a subsistence operation which is dependent on meagre and often diminishing scarce resources on small farms. There are also the various types of constraints to production on small farms (Chapter 6) that further affect integrated systems.

Additionally, integrated systems demand more initiative, inter-sectoral effort and inter-disciplinary approaches, greater resourcefulness and commitment, willingness to be innovative and access to information and technical know-how, all of which can be serious deterrents. The only exception to this is the pig-fish-duck-vegetable system (see Chapter 7).

For these reasons, the development of integrated systems has been hampered by inadequate national and donor support in the past. The situation is however changing and there is increasing appreciation of and support for such systems, in view of their wider benefits in terms of efficiency of natural resource use, nutrient recycling, environmental protection and sustainable development. Such efforts need to be accelerated, especially in South-East Asia where the potential for such development is obvious and where there has been a tradition of using such systems on small farms.

INTEGRATED PIG-DUCKS-FISH-VEGETABLE SYSTEMS

With specific reference to fish, integration with pigs, ducks and vegetables is a time-honoured practice in which meagre resources are effectively used interactively to maximize protein production. In recent years, recognition of the importance of ruminants, both in terms of production and the value of their manure, has led to efforts to explore the integration of other systems with fish production. The potential benefits are increased efficiency of use of the existing crop and animal resources, reduced dependence on purchased concentrates for feeding fish and a concurrent reduction in costs of feeding and production. The efficiency of nitrogen utilization for fish biomass production is relatively higher in systems where concentrates are used but the use of nitrogenous manure from animals causes less pollution.

These systems have been widely practised in China, Vietnam and Cambodia but, surprisingly, the different systems, individual components, interactions between them and the effects on the environment, economic analysis, socio-economic benefits on farm households and issues of sustainability do not appear to have been studied and documented.

INTEGRATED SYSTEMS INVOLVING VARIOUS ANIMALS

Unlike the traditional integrated system involving pigs, ducks, fish and vegetables that is more widely known, the inclusion of ruminants into such systems is relatively new. There are several reasons for this, chief of which is the fact that ruminants, unlike pigs and ducks, are not normally reared adjacent to ponds but rather in extensive grazing systems. Secondly, and related to this, extensive systems do not enable easy concentration and collection of dung from animals in sizeable amounts for use in fish ponds, unless the animals are maintained in stall-fed systems. Thirdly, feedlots that provide a large supply of dung for use by fish are relatively uncommon in South-East

Asia, which has also not encouraged the development of integrated systems combining fish and animals.

These limitations are also reflected in the very limited research into such systems and, associated with this, the failure to develop suitable methodology to promote such enterprises. Figure 10 illustrates the integration of animals (ruminants and non-ruminants) with crops, pigs and fish. The crops referred to are mainly annual crops like cassava, maize, groundnuts, rice and sweet potatoes.

It is not surprising therefore that results from such integrated systems, and the effects of interactions of the components (crops, fish and individual animal species) are scarce. This has also prevented the identification of which animal species fits best into such integrated systems.

One of the few studies of this type concerns the integration of goats and ducks with fish in Malaysia. A 30-40% increase in growth rate has been reported in this system in which the performance of grass carp was also superior to that of big head carp (Mukherjee, 1985).

In the ponds, several water weeds are invariably present, a very good example of which is water hyacinth (*Eichhornia crassipes*) which has been used for feeding both pigs and ruminants (Devendra, 1988). The special features of this type of integrated system are:

- The complementary role of ruminants to utilize non-marketable crop residues in *situ*, the manure production being used by fish, whereby the meagre resources are put to more effective use.
- Availability of water plants which can also be simultaneously utilized by ruminants.
- Reduced cost of feeding and production due to more intensive use of available indigenous feeds.
- Demonstrable benefits in terms of significant income generation from the sale of crops, animals, fish and some by-products like rice-bran in rice-based systems.
- Development of sustainable integrated systems combining fish and animals.

Figure 10. Relationships between crop-animal interactions and fish production.

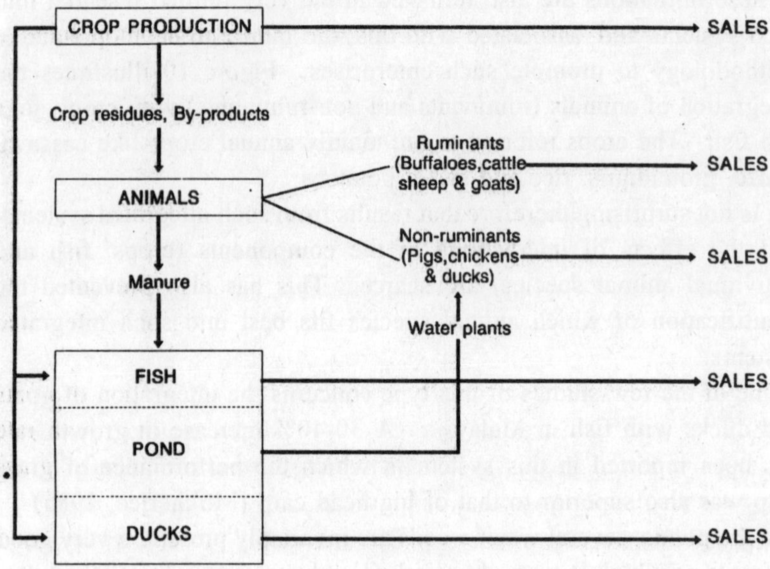

THE SIGNIFICANCE OF MANURE FROM ANIMALS

The quality and amount of manure produced from animals influences the development as well as the efficiency of integrated systems. The amount of manure produced by individual animal species, and hence the nitrogen contribution, is mainly a function of type of species, size, age, sex, feeding regime and also health of the animals. Table 8.1 provides an indication of the relative contribution by individual species on the assumption that these are only meat producing animals and that they are stall-fed

Table 8.1 Relative dung and nitrogen production in different animal species (per head/day)

Species	Adult live weight (kg)	Dung production (kg DM)	N content (%)*	N production (g)*	N production/ year (kg)*
Buffalo	460.0	5.8	0.80	46.40	16.90
Cattle	350.0	4.4	0.73	32.10	11.70
Goat	20.0	0.3	1.32	4.00	1.50
Sheep	20.0	0.3	0.91	2.70	1.00
Chicken	2.0	0.05	3.90	0.20**	0.07
Ducks	3.0	0.06	3.00	0.18**	0.07

* On dry matter basis
** In mg

It is clear that there are distinct qualitative and quantitative difference between the manures produced by individual species (Mueller, 1980). In particular, attention is drawn to differences in the N content in the faeces. With ruminants in general, the distribution of N in faeces and urine is approximately the same but, with non-ruminants, the percentage of N is higher in urine. Smith, Calvert and Menear (1973) reported for instance that pigs and poultry had 33-67% total N in faeces and 25-75% in urine. Additionally, there is also the issue of differential rates of N breakdown between different types of faeces. Goat manure for example has contains biuret from which ammonia is more slowly released (Devendra, 1983).

PRODUCTIVITY OF FISH

Nitrogenous manure inputs clearly influence the productivity of fish in ponds. Quantitative studies on this are limited and in any case usually restricted to the involvement of individual animal species.

In an effort to overcome the difficulties of comparing data from various workers, Edwards (1983) attempted to estimate the number of pigs, dairy cows and buffaloes required to produce a mean yield of

174.7 kg of fish/200m²/year from the manure of 26.7 ducks (equivalent to an extrapolated yield of 8735 kg/ha/year from 1335 ducks). The number of animals required to produce this quantity of fish per 200m²/year was approximately 8 pigs, 1 dairy cow and 2 swamp buffaloes. Table 8.2 presents the details of this calculation.

Table 8.2 Estimated number of pigs, dairy cows and buffaloes required to produce the same yield of 174.7 kg of fish/200m²/yr, as 26.7 ducks based on equivalent nitrogen manure inputs to the fish pond (Edwards, 1983).

Livestock	Manure production (kg DM/animal/year)	N content (%)	Livestock (no./ 200m² pond/year)	Livestock (no./ha/year)
Laying duck	20.6	2.5	26.7	1335
Pig	178.0	1.9	8.2	410
Dairy cow	784.0	2.2	0.8	40
Buffalo	750.0	1.1	1.7	85

FUTURE OF INTEGRATED SYSTEMS INVOLVING PONDS

The future of integrated systems is dependent on the following:

- Demand for animal products and market outlets.
- Type of ruminant species, numbers and management system (semi-intensive *v.* intensive).
- Type and quantity of available feeds, especially crop residues.
- Access to availability of tree fodders for utilization by ruminants, e.g., *Leucaena leucocephala*, *Gliricidia sepium* and *Sesbania grandiflora*.
- Reduced availability of land for grazing and the development of more intensive stall-feeding systems.
- Type and amount of manure available from animals.
- Rising cost of feed and feed formulation.
- Access to ponds and water supply.

INTEGRATED SMALL RUMINANTS-TREE CROPPING SYSTEMS

The importance of small ruminants in integrated systems is becoming increasing recognition in several countries in South-East Asia (see Chapter 7). However, the process of integration and the methodology for this remain to be fully developed. There are also issues of the effects on the parent crop and also the effects of crops on animals that need to be analyzed.

Effects of animal integration on the parent crop

A wide variety of issues must be considered in this complex interaction. The following are not listed in any particular order of priority but refer to a number of important examples. It is by no means an exhaustive list.

- Possible damage to leaves or bark of the primary tree by the grazing or browsing animal. Greater precautions must be taken in introducing goats into rubber plantations because of possible damage to bark. Young coconut, oil-palm and rubber trees are more susceptible to browsing.
- The beneficial effects of the animal in weed control and reductions in herbicide use and costs.
- Beneficial effect of the animal in browsing lower, senescent leaves.
- Possible transmission of plant diseases from pasture plants to the trees.
- Soil compaction by grazing animals.
- Soil organic matter and nitrogen fertilizer from animal excreta and urine.
- Soil moisture depletion by the forage crop. Higher evaporation rates occur if ground cover is overgrazed.
- Animal damage to latex collection cups in rubber cultivation.
- Possible reduction of rodent population (important in oil-palm plantations) with grazing.

Effects of primary crop management on small ruminants

The following issues are relevant to the effects of primary crop management on the animals. These issues merit continuous monitoring and research.

- The residual effect of herbicides (contact *v.* systemic) and its duration.
- Adjusting grazing rotations to cultural and harvesting practices. Indigestion and death of the animals as a result of latex consumption may be a problem on rubber plantations. Problems of metabolic disorder or even nutrition imbalances are also likely with the ingestion of fruitlets of oil-palm fruit bunches, rubber leaves and seeds.
- Possible effects in areas where rodenticides have been used or discharged (for example, palm-oil mill effluent) on the land and in streams; there are also the effects of oil-palm by-products build-up.
- Mineral imbalances and toxicities are likely to be a problem. A case in point concerns copper levels which can be as high as 30-35 ppm (well above the recommended limit for small ruminants).

Most of the animal-related issues are common to other intensive, mixed crop-livestock farms. However, the following are unique to the tree crop-livestock association.

- Time of introduction of animals is critical so as not to cause damage to the parent crop with reduction in yield and serious economic consequences. With oil palm for example, the optimum time for introduction is four to five years of age to avoid any damage to the leaves.
- Intensity of grazing and carrying capacity will be affected by the space occupied by the trees and the amount of light penetrating the canopy.
- Fencing and/or shepherding of animals will be influenced by labour availability and, on large estates, by requirements for movement of machinery.

- Many by-products from tree crop processing are readily available and potentially valuable for ruminant feeding and strategic supplementation. These are coconut: coconut meal; oil palm: palm press fibre, palm kernel cake, palm oil mill effluent (POME); and rubber: rubber seed meal. In addition to these, there are other non-conventional feed resources such as cassava leaves (*Manihot esculenta*) which are also extensively used in these situations (Devendra, 1985).
- There are a number of important management-related issues which include: the use of tree legumes such as *Leucaena leucocephala* and *Sesbania grandiflora* as feeds, fuel and as a fenceline; supplementation; provision of water and mineral licks; conservation of crop residues and forages for dry season use; hours of available grazing per day; control of predators; labour availability; complementarity of sheep and goats and possibly also cattle in mixed grazing systems; manipulation of the breeding season to take best advantage of seasonal feed availability; type and regularity of drenching; and housing requirements.
- The animal health problems of major importance include endoparasites (especially in grazing systems), ectoparasites (eg. scabies) and respiratory diseases such as pleuropneumonia. These need to be regularly monitored and appropriate control measures adopted, for example, regular drenching.

INTEGRATED SYSTEM BASED ON SUGAR CANE

Elsewhere, in Colombia, an example of an integrated farming system is based on sugar cane and forage trees, fractionated to provide feed for pigs and poultry (the juice and tree leaves), sheep (the cane tops and tree leaves), fuel for the family (bagasse and firewood) and litter for sheep and earthworms (bagasse), with recycling of excreta through biodigesters to provide fuel (biogas) and fertilizer (the effluent) for water plants in ponds and for crops (Preston, 1990). Figure 11 illustrates the model. The system has considerable merit especially in situations where biomass production from sugar cane is high such as in the Philippines, Vietnam and Malaysia.

Figure 11. Integrated system based on sugarcane (Preston 1990).

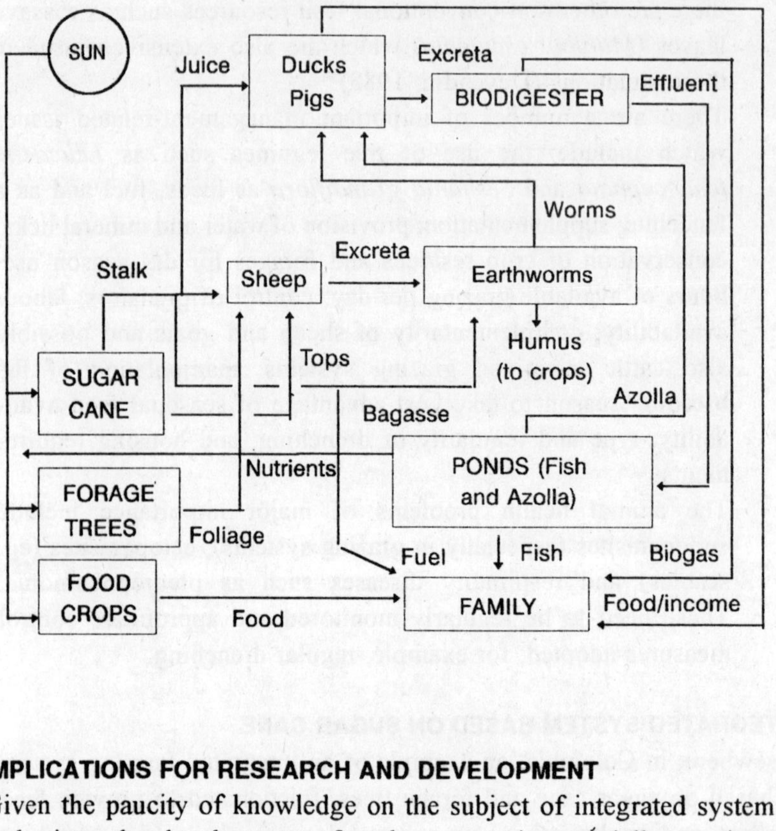

IMPLICATIONS FOR RESEARCH AND DEVELOPMENT

Given the paucity of knowledge on the subject of integrated systems and, since the development of such systems is especially consistent with sustainability, efficient management of natural resources and environmental protection, a high priority needs to be accorded to the formulation of research and development on this subject, backed by institutional and government support for such programmes. The following are some of the areas that merit attention:

- Relevance and rationale for choice of animal component(s).
- Inter-disciplinary approaches which include inter-commodity participatory links between animal and fish scientists.
- Increased efficiency of utilization of existing limited resources within small farm systems, requiring carefully selected integration of the components (crops, animals and fish)
- An understanding of the role of each component, interactions between them and the development of methodology to support measurements.
- A strong systems perspective, complete with the different stages (diagnosis, design, testing and on-farm application and extension) that will enhance research programmes.
- The efficiency of utilization of nutrients and the relative contribution of the components of the system.
- Socio-economic analysis is essential to provide diagnosis of the circumstances and changes, including the elements of processing, utilization and marketing.
- The systems approach will also enable an assessment of sustainability and environmental effects, as well as economic impact.

Chapter 9

The framework for development of integrated systems

The framework for integrated systems development needs to take into consideration several facets of programme development and delivery. Essentially these relate to problem definition, priority setting, definition of a research and development agenda, timeframe for the work and an operational strategy. Together these need to ensure that the work to be undertaken is pragmatic, relevant to the search for solutions, can contribute to progress and has the potential for sustainable development.

In a general sense, there needs to be an initial systems approach to assess the issues in specific agro-ecosystems, the nature and extent of the complex interactions between the environment, crops and animals, and the formulation of strategies and interventions that can provide solutions.

Concerning animals, there needs to be an understanding of the species found, breeds used, major constraints and an awareness of the problems of producers and consumers.

CRITERIA FOR PROJECT FORMULATION

Project formulation and development needs to consider several criteria and involve different commodities (e.g., crops, animals, forestry and fish culture) and disciplines (animal nutrition, agronomy, sociology and economics) as appropriate. The approach needs to be flexible, in order to select and modify the team composition based on the needs of the work. The team finally assembled will thus be able to cope with the needs of the work and, more importantly, contribute to the formulation of the research and development required, as well as ensure successful implementation and completion.

The criteria for such support takes cognisance of the following factors:

- Relevance, applicability and suitability of integration with existing resources on small farms.
- Clear definition of the nature and magnitude of problems associated with integration.
- Research requirements, e.g., crop-animal interactions, and the effects of these on the farm.
- Nature and importance of the problems.
- Capacity to use available natural resources fully.
- Timely intervention and completion of research within the time-frame.
- Clear identification of systems and commodities (eg. rice, pigs and fish) in order to promote efficient resource management, conservation and a sound environment.
- Clear definition of potential users and target populations. Participation of farmers is central.
- Potential benefits (optimization of income and renewability), impact, contribution to solutions, economic and social costs.
- Lessening of the imbalance in development between rural and urban people.
- Contribution to the alleviation of rural nutrition and poverty.
- National and regional development goals.
- Contribution to the development of sustainable crop-animal systems.
- Regional relevance, i.e., possibility of transfer of technology and replication without any negative impact.

The above criteria are extremely important in the assessment of project support for research and development. Essentially, the project must be useful in improving the living standards of people, will use natural resources fully, is consistent with national development goals, and has regional applicability. The latter implies that the research findings are likely to be applicable in other countries in South-East Asia and elsewhere.

An important dimension concerning project development is detailed assessment of the socio-economic relevance of prevailing practices on small farms. With animals, for example, this approach implies detailed investigations of patterns of production, contribution to income and human nutrition, constraints, perceptions of farmers, marketing aspects and economic potential. This kind of work needs to consider year-round and seasonal differences.

RESOURCE REQUIREMENTS

The resource requirements need to include all aspects of what it takes to execute the work. Often the overall requirements are in two parts:

- Detailed assessment of the real needs through surveys or feasibility studies for purposes of precise problem definition and formulation of research and development agenda.
- Complete requirements for implementation: operational needs, inputs (e.g., feeds and fertilisers), local and international travel costs, equipment, wages, training, communication and costs of disseminating the information generated.

CONSERVATION OF ON-FARM GENETIC BIO-DIVERSITY

The animal genetic resources of Asia are characterized by their great diversity. A wide range of resources are found on the small farms of South-East Asia and their conservation is essential. Conservation implies detailed characterization using both published and unpublished information, as well as clear definition of the genetic attributes of individual animal species and breeds which are unique to the region. It is equally important to describe the environment to which the species or breed is adapted, in order to determine and predict the genetic performance specific to this location.

The conservation of on-farm genetic bio-diversity has received inadequate attention in the past and their is a need to improve and maintain the indigenous breeds. More importantly, these breeds are being threatened by indiscriminate crossbreeding with extensive importation of exotic breeds, not all of which are necessarily advantageous. The development of artificial insemination and other techniques that facilitate easy transfer of breeding material across regions has resulted in the replacement of indigenous breeds and the dilution and loss of identifiable animal genetic bio-diversity (Chapter 6). This is evident, for example, with several Chinese breeds of pigs, the Katjang goat breed in Indonesia and the Kedah-Kelantan cattle of Malaysia. Conservation is thus essential for reasons of economic potential, scientific use and also cultural interest.

There is a need therefore for more aggressive programmes that can conserve animal genetic resources. It is essential however, that such programmes are undertaken without hindering the activities of small farm systems, taking into account the meagre resources available and the main objectives of generating income and producing food for their livelihood.

INSTITUTIONAL REQUIREMENTS

The institutional requirements for supporting the work are many:

- Commitment to the concept of integrated systems and a systems approach.
- Provision of manpower and support services for the duration of the project.
- Support for training, both formal and informal.
- Information exchange services.
- Dissemination of information.

The formulation and implementation of the project within the time-frame will be mainly carried out by the national institution. Funding can come from national sources and/or external donors. The management of the project becomes an institutional responsibility from implementation, management of data (research and financial) and analysis of results and impact.

In addition to the above, there are other aspects that institutions must address in the context of developing sustainable small farm systems:

- Indigenous technologies must be adapted to the needs of small farmers.

- Closer links are required between the micro-economic perceptions of small farmers and macro-economic government policies.
- Government policies and national research systems need to identify integrated agricultural production with the protection of natural resources, regulation and control of interventions and support services for rural people and various levels of training. Cooperative movement and the development of cooperatives greatly enhance the success of production, marketing and processing systems and foster self-reliance.
- Private sector participation in agricultural production and marketing activities with community-based decision making and management of local affairs, including common property issues. Associated with this, much more can be done for poor farming families to improve access to agricultural services, inputs and also credit
- For active community-based participation, the necessary structures should be in place.
- An effective communication system is necessary to facilitate the diffusion of practical technical innovations, communicate price policies, fluctuations and market dynamics, potential processing opportunities and linkages with other sectors.
- Formal and informal education systems, focused on human resource development, should be identified with the objectives of sound resource management, conservation of the environment and the development of sustainable agriculture.
- Agricultural extension programmes to serve the needs of farmers should be based on the integration of research and development activities that are needs-oriented and include the results and experiences of farmers.
- Mechanisms for inter-institutional coordination and collaboration need to be considerably strengthened within the framework of consultation and sharing.

POLICY SUPPORT

Appropriate policy must be in place to catalyze the project at all levels, from formulation, implementation and monitoring to the analysis of results and impact. Policy decisions are thus important to provide a framework for the systems approach and in support of resource development strategies.

IMPLEMENTATION

Once the project has been carefully formulated, wide inter-institutional discussion and consultation, appropriate linkages and support services must also be defined. Implementation is the next step and it is essential that the objectives of the project are set within a defined timeframe which involves regular monitoring. The final step is detailed analysis of the results, extent of adoption and evalution of the impact.

Some items that will warrant attention during the course of the project are:

- Initial preparatory work should involve the participation of the project team and farmers.
- Pragmatism and urgency are essential features.
- Timing may be crucial depending on seasonality where this can be a problem, e.g., onset of dry or wet periods.
- Flexibility to enable changes to meet adaptive needs due to locational and operational problems at the farm level, without compromising statistical validity.
- Preparedness for and commitment to more sustained effort and time inputs as appropriate.

CRITERIA FOR EVALUATION

If appropriate technology is to be adopted, then the acceptance and benefits need to be evaluated in terms of technical (e.g., efficiency ratios, yield/unit input), economic (e.g., net income, cost-benefit ratios, gross margin, internal rate of return, factor share of total output, value-added income) and socio-cultural acceptability (e.g., rate and number of adopters, quality-of-life assessments). There are two key elements in this. Firstly, continuous monitoring of the progress of the project throughout its duration is required and should also be defined at the start of the project. Secondly, parameters to assess impact are necessary. These include the following:

- Cost-benefit analysis.
- Before-and-after trends.
- Environmental accounting.

The research and development objectives of the project thus need to include economic and social parameters, optimization of income, renewability and self-reliance. These aspects are consistent with the goals of sustainable agriculture and a sound environment in which the efficient use and management of the natural resources is implicit.

IMPACT ANALYSIS

It is essential that every stage of the development of integrated farming systems: project formulation, resource requirements, institutional support, implementation and evaluation, is finally assessed in terms of impact of the total effort. The measurement of impact is essential to assess the efficiency of the mode and approach to resource utilization, the negative and positive effects, lessons learnt and cost- effectiveness. The criteria fall into two categories: firstly, those which allude to the direct consequences on farm households and, secondly, indirecct benefits of changes in the overall research systems where the work is conducted (Anderson, 1985).

There is a paucity of information on impact analysis at present and, in view of the importance attached to resource utilization, this aspect needs much more study in the future with a focus on the different types of integrated crop-animal systems and their contribution to sustainable development.

Chapter 10
Conclusions

Small farm systems combining various crops and animals will continue to remain the backbone of agriculture and sustain the livelihoods of several millions of poor farmers in South-East Asia within the foreseeable future. The natural resource base, with its reservoir of plants and animal populations, will be expected to provide the bulk of the food required to support increasing human populations. Small farms have contributed to this need in the past and will continue to do so in the future.

Increased food production and alleviation of poverty in the long term will not be without costs and effects on the use of the natural resource base as well as the environment. The challenging task for the future is how these goals can be achieved in a manner involving a more efficient, low-input, sustainable agriculture. It is likely to make use of indigenous knowledge systems in which there is reduced dependency on chemicals, maintenance of soil fertility, integrated pest management and conservation of on-farm genetic biodiversity. The overall development priority is to make small farms more sustainable and profitable through appropriate technological interventions and policy adjustments.

The farmers' first priority is to increase income and feed their families. Policy adjustments must thus consider a balance of environmental and social issues and formulate proposals in a manner that can be supportive of small farmers and their efforts.

The more efficient use of natural resources will involve the adoption of appropriate technologies which generate profits for farmers and spearhead agricultural growth. Mechanisms to encourage greater use of such technologies, methods of diffusion, delivery and acceptance by farmers will assume far greater importance in the future. The onus is initially on the scientist and policy makers to facilitate this process which, if well organised and delivered through participatory processes, has the advantage in the long term of making the farmers themselves into both the managers and beneficiaries of new technology. Constraints on the adoption of new technologies will need to be addressed and overcome in order to balance the immediate food security needs of farmers and the longer term agricultural growth and conservation goals. Research is also required to provide a better understanding and definition of the links between poverty, natural resource use and management, indigenous knowledge systems and institutions.

Rising human populations and decreased availability of land will demand more intensive production systems and this will increase the pressure on natural resources. This will highlight the importance of integrated systems of food production that maintain environmental integrity.

In Asia, there is already a good understanding of small farm systems. It began with a specific focus on crops in the 1970's and has now been extended to crop-animal systems during the last decade. This has in turn led to a better understanding of the role and nature of involvement of animals in integrated systems, and the development of appropriate research protocols and methodologies that can assess the extent of the contribution made by animals. This aspect however is very much in its infancy and will need even greater attention in the future.

The systems approach has been extremely useful in the past in enabling a good understanding of farming systems. Given the complexity of the issues, the new development imperatives and the dynamic nature of farming systems, further progress will require more changes in methodology in the future. The following issues adapted from Chambers (1991) and Zandstra (1991) constitute the challenges for the future:

- Sustainable development will require more intensive and complex farming systems and methodologies to support it.
- Participation of farmers is essential, from the development of the

research agenda through to on-farm application.

- The balance of advantage shifts from scientists to farmers in managing complexity, in exploring diversity, in experimenting and in innovation.
- Rural people can manifest greater analytical capabilities than outside professionals have supposed.
- Increased environmental concerns must be combined with gender-differentiated technology development and new agricultural policies.
- The sustainability of systems must be monitored

The challenges facing animal production in the future will be especially critical since questions and doubts linger about its efficiency, contribution and inability to meet national targets. These concerns now need to be more closely identified with issues concerning the environment, efficient natural resource use and management, and sustainability. Strategies must therefore address not only increased contribution from animals in the future, but also enable them to make a parallel ecological and socio-economic impact. Sustainable animal production within integrated small farm systems in South-East Asia offers considerable potential to meet the challenges and development imperatives of the future.

References

Adams, D. and Coward, E.W. 1972. *Small farmer development strategies.* Agricultural Development Council, New York, 6pp.

Anderson, J.R. 1985. Assessing the impact of farming systems research: framework and problems. Agricultural Administration 20: 225-235.

Anderson, J.R. 1991. What is the nature of the food problem? *Outlook on Agriculture* 20: 213-218.

Amir, P. and Knipscheer, H.C. 1989. *Conducting On-farm Animal Research: Procedures Economic Analysis.* Winrock International and International Development Research Centre (IDRC), Singapore, 244 pp.

Arga, I.W. 1990. Socio-economic aspects of the three strata forage system in Bali. In: *Shrubs and Tree Fodders for Farm Animals* (Ed. C. Devendra). IDRC-27e. International Development Research Centre, Ottawa, Canada, pp. 118-129.

Carangal, V. R., Tengco, P.L., Miah, N.I. and Topak-Ngarm, A. 1988. Food-feed crop inter-cropping under rainfed lowland conditions. *Proceedings of the IIIrd Crop-Animal Systems Research Workshop.* International Rice Research Institute, Los Banos, Philippines, pp. 435-451.

Chambers, R. 1991. Complexity, diversity and competence: towards sustainable livelihood from farming systems in the 21st Century. *Journal of the Asian Farming Systems Association* 1: 79-89.

Chantalakhana, C. 1980. An overview of the major constraints and some solutions in livestock development in South East Asia. *Proceedings of an International Workshop on Feeds and Feeding of Livestock and Poultry Feed Composition.* Data Documentation and Feeding Systems in the APHCA region, Manila, Philippines, pp. 13-28.

Chantalakhana, C. 1990. Small farm animal production and sustainable agriculture. *Proceedings of the 5th AAAP Animal Science Congress.* Taipei, Taiwan. Vol. 2, 39-58.

CRIC. 1991. *Crop-animal systems. Phase II.* Terminal Report. Bogor, Indonesia.

Davis, C.H. 1983. Experiences in Bangladesh with improving the nutritive value of straw. In: *The*

Utilisation of Fibrous Agricultural Residues as Animal Feeds. Australian Government Publishing Service, Canberra, Australia, pp. 123-128.

Devendra, C. 1979a. *Malaysian Feedingstuffs.* Malaysian Agricultural Research and Development Institute, Serdang, Selangor, Malaysia, 145 pp.

Devendra, C. 1979b. Goat and sheep production potential in the ASEAN region. *World Animal Review* 32: 33-41.

Devendra, C. 1982. Small farmer goat production in the less developed countries. *Proceedings of the 3rd International Conference on Goat Production and Disease.* Tucson Arizona, U.S.A, pp. 329-330.

Devendra, C. 1983. Small farm systems combining crops and animals. *Proceedings of the World Conference on Animal Production.* Tokyo, Japan. Vol. I, pp. 173-191.

Devendra, C. 1984. Prospects for processing and treatments of crop residues and agro-industrial by-products for ruminants in the Asian region. *Proceedings of a Conference on Feeds and Feeding Systems for Livestock.* 8th Annual Conference of the Malaysian Society of Animal Production (Eds. R.I. Hutagalung, V.F. Hew, C. Devendra and P. Vijuchulata) Gentings Highlands, Malaysia, pp. 25-36.

Devendra, C. 1985. Integrated farming systems involving small ruminants. *Proceedings of the 3rd Asian-Australasian Animal Science Congress,* Seoul, Korea. Vol. 1, pp. 146-155.

Devendra, C. 1987. Herbivores in the arid and wet tropics. In: *The Nutrition of Herbivores* (Eds. J.B. Hacker and J.H. Ternouth). Academic Press, Sydney, Australia, pp. 23-46.

Devendra, C. 1988. Forage supplements: nutritional significance and utilisation for draught, meat and milk production in buffaloes. *Proceedings of the IInd World Buffalo Congress.* Indian Council of Agricultural Research. Vol. 2, pp. 409-423.

Devendra, C. 1989. Ruminant production systems in developing countries: resource utilisation. In: *Feeding Strategies for Improved Productivity of Ruminant Livestock in Development Countries.* IAEA, Vienna, pp. 5-30.

Devendra, C. 1990a. The use of shrubs and tree fodders by ruminants. In: *Shrubs and Tree Fodders for Farm Animals* (Ed. C. Devendra). IDRC-276e. International Development Research Centre, Ottawa, Canada, pp. 42-60.

Devendra, C. 1990b. Fibrous crop residues: strategies for the efficient use and development of feeding systems. *Proceedings of the ICAR/Netherlands Workshop on Fibrous Crop Residues in Crop-Animal Systems.* Karnal, India. (In press).

Devendra, C. 1991a. Integrated animal-fish-mixed cropping systems. *Proceedings of an FAO International Workshop on Integrated Fish Production Systems.* Kuala Lumpur, Malaysia. (In press).

Devendra, C. 1991b. The potential for integration of small ruminants and tree cropping systems in South and South-East Asia. *World Animal Review* 66: 13-22.

Devendra, C. 1992a. Goats and rural prosperity. *Pre-Conference Proceedings. Vth International Conference on Goats.* New Delhi, India, pp. 6-25.

Devendra, C. 1992b. *Non-conventional feed resources in Asia and the Pacific. Strategies for expanding utilisation at the small farm level.* 4th Revised Edn. RAPA/FAO, Bangkok, Thailand, 170 pp.

Devendra, C. and Chantalakhana, C. 1992. Development of sustainable crop-animal systems in Asia. *Proceedings of the VIth Asian-Australasian Animal Science Congress* (Eds. Bunyavejchewin, P., Sangdid, S. and Hangsanet, K.). Bangkok, Thailand. Vol. 1, pp. 21-40.

Devendra C. and Fuller, M.F. 1979. *Pig Production in the Tropics.* Oxford University Press, Oxford, England, 172 pp.

Devendra, C. and Lee, T.K.C. 1975. Studies on Kedah-Kelantan cattle. Effect of improved nutrition on growth. *MARDI Research Bulletin* 3: 68-86.

Doyle, P.T., Devendra, C. and Pearce, G.R. 1985. *Rice Straw as a Feed for Ruminants.* International Development Program of Australian Universities and Colleges, Canberra, Australia., 117 pp.

Duckham, A.M. and Masefield, O.D. 1970. *Farming Systems of the World.* Chatto and Windus, London.

Edwards, P. 1983. The future potential of integrated farming systems in Asia. *Proceedings of the Vth World Conference on Animal Production.* Vol. 1, pp. 273-281.

Edwards, P., Pullin, R.S.V. and Gartner, J.A. 1988. *Research and education for the development of crop-livestock-fish farming systems in the tropics.* ICLARM Studies and Reviews. No. 16, 53 pp.

FAO. 1980. *The classification of world livestock systems.* Typescript, 37pp.

FAO. 1989. *Production Year*book. Vol. 43. FAO, Rome, Italy.

FAO. 1990. *Production Year*book. Vol. 44. FAO, Rome, Italy.

FAO. 1991. *Agrostat database.* FAO, Rome, Italy.

FAO/RAFE. 1978. FAO Regional Office for Asia and the Far East. Bangkok, Thailand. pp. 72-77.

FAO/UNDP. 1976. Regional Office for Asia and the Far East, Bangkok, Thailand. (Mimeograph), 66 pp.

Giaever, H. 1984. The economics of using straw on feed. In: *Straw and Other Fibrous By-products as*

Feed. (Eds. F. Sundstøl and E. Owen). Elsevier, Ansterdam, The Netherlands, pp. 588-574.

Greenhalgh, J.F.D. 1984. Upgrading crop and agricultural by-products for animal production. In: *Herbivore Nutrition in the Sub-tropics and Tropics* (Eds. F.M.C. Gilchrist and R.I. Machie). The Science Press (Pte) Ltd., Craightall, South Africa, pp. 167-184.

Harris, L.S., Leche, T.F., Kearl, L.C., Fonnesbeck, P.V. and Lloyd, H. 1982. *Central and South East Asia Tables of Feed Composition*. International Feedstuffs Institute, Logan, Utah, U.S.A., 513 pp.

Hartadi, H., Redsohadiprodjo, S., Lebdosukojo, S., Tillman, A., Kearl, L.C. and Harris, L.S. 1980. *Tables of Feed Composition for Indonesia*. International Feedstuffs Institute, Logan, Utah, U.S.A., 145 pp.

Holm, J. 1971. *Feeding Tables*. Livestock Breeding Station. Huey Kaew, Chieng Mai, Thailand, 23 pp.

Ibrahim, M.N.M., Fernando, D.N.S. and Fernando, S.N.F.M. 1984. Evaluation of different methods of urea-ammonia treatment for use at the village level. In: *The Utilisation of Fibrous Agricultural Residues as Animal Feeds* (Ed. P.T. Doyle), School of Agriculture and Forestry, University of Melbourne, Parkville, Victoria, Australia, pp. 131-139.

Knipscheer, H.C., de Boer, J., Sabrani, M., Soedjana, T. 1983. The economic role of sheep and goats in Indonesia: A case study in West Java. *Bulletin of Economic Studies* 19: 74-93.

Kunju, P.J.G. 1986. Urea-molasses block licks: a feed supplement for ruminants. In: *Rice straw and Related Feeds in Ruminant Rations* (Eds. M.N.M. Ibrahim and J.B. Schiere), Proceedings of an International Workshop, Kandy, Sri Lanka, pp. 261-274.

Lana, K., Nitis, I.M., Suarna, K., Putra, K. and Sukhanten, K. 1990. Research protocols appropriate to the development of methodology for the three-strata forage system. In: *Shrubs and Tree Fodders for Farm Animals* (Ed. C. Devendra). IDRC-27e, International Development Research Centre, Ottawa, Canada, pp. 103-117.

Leng, R.A., Preston, T.R., Sansoucy, R. and Kunju, P.J.G. 1991. Multinutrient blocks as a strategic supplement for ruminants. *World Animal Review* 67: 11-20.

McDowell, R.E. and Hilderbrand, P.H. 1980. Integrated crop and animal production: making the most of resources available to small farmers in developing countries. *Rockefeller Foundation Conference*, Bellagio, Italy (Mimeograph).

Mahadevan, P. 1984. Education of livestock producers and agents of change in the use of new technology. In: *Development of Animal Production Systems* (Ed. B. Nestel). World Animal Science Series A2,

Elsevier Scientific Publishing Co., The Netherlands, pp. 107-108.

Mahadevan, P. and Devendra, C. 1986. Present and projected ruminant production systems of South-East Asia and the South Pacific. In: *Forages in South-East Asia and the Pacific*. ACIAR Proceedings, No. 12 pp. 1-6.

Mueller, Z.O. 1980. *Feed from animal wastes.* FAO Animal Production Health Paper No. 18, 190 pp.

Mukherjee, T.K. 1985. Integration of aquaculture and livestock farming; an experimental study for rural development. *Proceedings of the II Asian Conference on Technology for Rural Development.* Kuala Lumpur, Malaysia, pp. 377-391.

Mukherjee, T.K. 1989. Development of goat breeds in Malaysia. *Asian Livestock* 14: 61-62.

Nitis, I.M., Lana, K., Sukanten, W., Suarna, M. and Putra, S. 1990. The concept and development of the three strata-forage system. In: *Shrubs and Tree Fodders for Farm Animals* (Ed. C. Devendra). IDRC-276e, International Development Research Centre, Ottawa, Canada, pp. 92-102.

Nuraini, K. 1990. Communication aspects of the three-strata forage system in Bali. In: *Shrubs and Tree Fodders for Farm Animals* (Ed. C. Devendra). IDRC-276e, International Development Research Centre, Ottawa, Canada, pp. 130-135.

Penafiel, S.R. and Veracion, V.P. 1987. *Goat raising in a pine forest in the Philippines: a case of a viable agro-forestry system.* South-East Asian Regional Centre for Graduate Study and Research in Agriculture, College, Laguna, Philippines, pp. 149-164.

Perdok, H.B., Muttettuwegama, G.S., Kaasehieter, G.A., Boon, H.M., van Wageningen, N.M., Arumugam, V., Linders, M.G. F.A. and Jayasuriya, M.C.N. 1984. Production response of lactating and growing ruminants fed urea-ammonia treated paddy straw with or without supplements. In: *The Utilisation of Fibrous Agricultural Residues as Animal Feeds* (Ed. P.T. Doyle). School of Agriculture and Forestry, University of Melbourne Printing Services, Parkville, Victoria, Australia, pp. 213-230.

Preston, T.R. 1990. Future strategies for livestock production in tropical third world countries. *Ambio* 19: 390-393.

Preston, T.R. and Leng, R.A. 1986. *Matching Ruminant Production Systems with Available Resources in the Tropics and Sub-Tropics.* Penambul Books, Armidale, Australia.

Putu, Gede, I. Fletcher and G.A. Riding. 1983. Effect of nutrition on ovarian activity in Indonesian swamp buffaloes. *Buffalo Bulletin* No. 2, 7 (Abstract).

RAPA/FAO, 1989. *Livestock development in Asia-Pacific region.*

RAPA/FAO Publication 1989/1, Bangkok, Thailand, 55 pp.

Ravallion, M., Datt, G. and Chen, S. 1992. *New estimates of aggregate poverty measures for the developing world, 1985-1989*. World Bank, Washington, D.C. U.S.A.

Remenyi, J.V. and McWilliam, J.R. 1986. Ruminant production trends in South-East Asia and the South Pacific and the need for forages. In: *Forages in South-East Asian and South Pacific Agriculture* (Eds. G.J. Blair, D.A. Ivory and T.R. Evans). ACIAR, Canberra, pp. 1-6.

Ruthenberg, H. 1976. *Farming Systems in the Tropics*. 2nd Edn. Clarendon Press, Oxford, 313 pp.

Sarma, J.S. and Yeung, P. 1985. *Livestock products in the third world: past trends and projections to 1990 and 2000*. International Food Policy Res. Institute Research Report No. 49, 87 pp.

Schiere, J.B. and Wieringa, J. 1988. Overcoming the nutritional limitations of rice straw for ruminants. Response of growing Sachiwal and local cross heifers to urea upgraded and urea supplementated straw. *Asian-Australasian Journal of Animal Science* 1: 209-212.

Smith, L.W., Calvert, C.C. and Menear, J.R. 1973. Dehydrated poultry manure as a protein supplement for sheep. *Proceedings of the Maryland Nutrition Conference*, pp. 35-42.

Soetanto, H. 1986. The use of molasses-urea blocks to provide supplements to sheep and goats. In: *The Utilisation of Fibrous Agricultural Residues as Animal Feeds*. (Ed. R.M. Dixon), School of Agriculture and Forestry, Univ. of Melbourne, Australia, pp. 231-238.

Spedding, C.R.W. 1975. *The Biology of Agricultural Systems*. Academic Press, London, England, 261 pp.

Steenwinkel, W.A. 1979. *Rural development and external assistance to that sector*. ILACO Symposium Arnhem, The Netherlands, pp. 77-94.

Topak-Ngarm, A., Aramada, E.C., Tengco, A. and Carangal, V.R. 1988. Food-forage intercropping under upland conditions. *Proceedings of a Crop-Animals Systems Research Workshop*, Serdang, Malaysia, pp. 453-472.

Turner, H.N. 1978. Some aspects of sheep breeding in the tropics. *World Animal Review* 28: 4-8.

Verma, M.L. 1983. Practical aspects of treatment of crop residues. In: *Utilisation of Fibrous Agricultural Residues as Animal Feeds*. (Ed. G.R. Pearce), Australian Government Publishing Service, Canberra, Australia, pp. 149-156.

Wapenham, W.A. 1979. *The big problem of the small farmer*. ILACO Symposium, Arnhem, The Netherlands, pp. 29-51.

Wong, C.C., Wan Hassan, W.E. and Tan, K.L. 1987. Milk production in Sachiwal X Friesian cows grazing on *Leucaena - Brachiaria decumbens* pasture with concentrate supplementation. *Proceedings of the Xth Annual Conference, Malaysian Society Animal Production* (Eds. R.I. Hutagalung, C.P. Chen, W.E. Wan Mohammed, A.T. Law and S. Sivarajasingam), pp. 280-286.

World Bank. 1992. *Development and the environment.* Oxford University Press, New York, U.S.A., 308 pp.

Zamora, R.G. and Baguio, S.S. 1984. *Feed Composition Tables for the Philippines.* PCARRD Book Series, No. 13, Philippine Council for Agriculture and Resources Research Development, Los Banos, Philippines, 264 pp.

Zandstra, H.G. 1991. Approaches in farming systems research and extension: problems and improvements. *Journal of the Asian Farming Systems Assocation* 1: 101-111.

APPENDIX 1

Table 1. Buffalo population ('000s) 1981-1991 (FAO, 1991)

Country	1981	1985	1991	Average annual growth rate (%)
Cambodia	880	974	1100	2.2
Indonesia	2488	3245	3500	3.8
Laos	879	974	1100	2.2
Malaysia	262	223	190	-2.9
Myanmar	1969	2143	2080	0.4
Philippines	2850	2983	2710	-0.6
Thailand	6120	6250	4743	-2.9
Vietnam	2316	2546	2929	2.4
Total	17292	18987	18011	0.3
As % of world population	14.1	13.7	13.2	1.3

Table 2. Cattle population ('000s) 1981-1991 (FAO, 1991)

Country	1981	1985	1991	Average annual growth rate (%)
Cambodia	956	1560	1950	8.6
Indonesia	6516	9526	10350	3.5
Laos	455	576	865	7.5
Malaysia	558	618	658	1.9
Myanmar	8857	9718	9310	0.4
Philippines	1940	1786	1677	-1.8
Thailand	4469	4829	6052	2.6
Vietnam	1664	2418	3282	7.5
Total	25414	31032	34343	2.7
As % of world population	2.1	2.4	2.7	0.4

Table 3. Goat population ('000s) 1981-1991 (FAO, 1991)

Country	1981	1985	1991	Average annual growth rate (%)
Indonesia	7790	9630	11300	4.0
Laos	54	67	143	10.6
Malaysia	360	336	315	-0.8
Myanmar	769	1195	1040	1.9
Philippines	1696	2191	2107	1.8
Thailand	38	81	140	11.7
Vietnam	173	300	450	10.6
Total	10879	13780	15495	3.6
As % of world population	2.4	2.8	3.0	1.7

Table 4. Sheep population ('000s) 1981-1991 (FAO, 1991)

Country	1981	1985	1991	Average annual growth rate (%)
Indonesia	4177	4890	5750	3.8
Malaysia	67	79	200	15.4
Myanmar	250	332	280	0.4
Philippines	30	30	30	0.0
Thailand	21	58	178	25.6
Total	4545	5389	6438	4.1
As % of world population	0.4	0.5	0.6	0.7

Table 5. Poultry population (millions) 1981-1991 (FAO, 1991)

Country	1981	1985	1991	Average annual growth rate (%)
Cambodia	3.5	5.8	7.7	8.4
Indonesia	185.6	331.2	590.0	12.5
Laos	5.6	7.8	8.0	3.3
Malaysia	52.0	95.0	148.0	12.4
Myanmar	27.2	32.7	24.0	-2.0
Philippines	57.7	52.4	65.5	1.3
Thailand	63.2	80.8	114.4	5.3
Vietnam	51.1	63.5	81.5	4.9
Total	445.9	6670.1	1039.1	9.1
As % of world population	6.3	6.8	10.3	4.4

Table 6. Duck population ('000s) 1981-1991 (FAO, 1991)

Country	1981	1985	1991	Average annual growth rate (%)
Cambodia	1620	2500	3500	8.7
Indonesia	22426	23870	29500	2.1
Laos	220	260	310	3.4
Malaysia	1450	3650	5000	12.4
Myanmar	4559	6110	3566	-4.1
Philippines	4783	5284	8268	5.0
Thailand	13387	14779	17300	2.7
Vietnam	23400	30000	28600	2.4
Total	71839	86463	96044	2.8
As % of world population	18.0	16.8	17.9	3.8

Table 7. Pig population ('000s) 1981-1991 (FAO, 1991)

Country	1981	1985	1991	Average annual growth rate (%)
Cambodia	260	1205	1610	16.6
Indonesia	3364	5560	6800	8.1
Laos	1176	1434	1390	1.2
Malaysia	2086	2111	2400	2.0
Myanmar	2196	3059	2250	1.1
Philippines	7758	7304	8007	0.2
Thailand	3616	4224	5000	2.7
Vietnam	10001	11760	12583	2.0
Total	30891	36555	40039	2.6
As % of world population	4.0	4.4	4.8	1.1

APPENDIX 2

Table 1. Meat and milk production by country in South-East Asia ('000 tonnes) (FAO, 1991)

Category	Cambodia	Indonesia	Laos	Malaysia	Myanmar	Philippines	Thailand	Vietnam	Total	Annual growth rate (%) (1981-1991)
Beef & veal	19.2	192.0	9.0	11.7	86.4	78.0	179.2	110.0	685.4	2.9
Buffalo meat	11.2	50.5	24.4	4.9	22.1	51.0	63.3	89.2	316.6	2.0
Mutton & lamb	-	44.0	-	0.1	1.6	0.1	0.6	-	464.8	5.6
Goat meat	33.8	54.0	0.5	0.5	5.1	2.6	0.7	3.4	90.6	2.1
Pig meat	35.8	295.0	54.0	194.5	82.5	710.0	340.0	850.0	2541.8	5.6
Duck meat	4.2	13.2	0.5	3.6	11.8	13.9	85.7	32.8	165.5	1.4
Poultry	21.0	445.0	24.8	348.0	69.6	222.0	630.0	135.0	1895.4	6.2
TOTAL MEAT	125.2	1093.7	113.2	563.3	279.1	1077.6	1299.5	1220.4	5741.9	3.7
Poultry eggs	13.5	400.0	34.0	211.5	34.7	267.0	127.6	100.0	258.9	4.8
Cow milk	17.0	329.4	9.6	29.5	456.3	15.2	178.0	39.5	1074.6	6.0
Buffalo milk	-	24.6	-	1.6	65.3	19.2	29.9	26.0	128.3	1.6
Other	-	180.0	-	-	5.6	-	-	-	254.6	4.1
TOTAL MILK	17.0	534.0	9.6	31.1	527.2	34.4	207.9	65.5	1457.5	4.2

Table 2. Production of wool and animal products in South-East Asia ('000 tonnes) (FAO, 1991)

Category	Cambodia	Indonesia	Laos	Malaysia	Myanmar	Philippines	Thailand	Vietnam	Total	Annual growth rate (%) (1981-1991)
Wool, greasy	-	17.3	-	0.2	0.3	-	-	-	17.5	3.4
Buffalo hides*	14.5	8.2	3.7	0.7	4.1	5.7	14.1	26.0	49.6	1.9
Cattle hides*	4.7	24.6	2.0	1.5	18.6	9.8	29.9	17.3	108.6	2.3
Goat skins*	-	10.8	-	0.1	0.7	5.6	0.1	0.6	17.9	2.0
Sheep skins*	-	8.8	-	-	0.3	-	10.5	-	19.6	10.4

* Fresh

APPENDIX 3

Table 1. Total meat consumption of livestock products in South-East Asia (kg/yr) (FAO, 1991))

Country	1980	1985	1990	Annual growth rate (%)
Cambodia	35	69	89	10.3
Indonesia	56	897	1181	8.0
Laos	78	107	110	3.4
Malaysia	315	450	638	8.4
Myanmar	244	299	273	1.4
Philippines	785	695	1128	2.7
Thailand	809	1023	1078	2.9
Vietnam	541	847	1156	7.1
Total	3297	4387	5653	5.5

Table 2. Total consumption of buffalo and cattle meat and products in South-East Asia (kg/yr) (FAO, 1991)

Country	1980	1985	1990	Annual growth rate (%)
Cambodia	17	25	29	5.4
Indonesia	201	279	306	4.9
Laos	27	36	32	2.0
Malaysia	32	47	68	7.5
Myanmar	93	99	106	1.4
Philippines	133	89	146	2.5
Thailand	214	224	234	0.8
Vietnam	103	136	192	6.7
Total	820	934	1113	3.5

Table 3. Total consumption of goat and sheep meat and products in South-East Asia (kg/yr) (FAO, 1991)

Country	1980	1985	1990	Annual growth rate (%)
Cambodia	-	-	-	-
Indonesia	63	76	83	1.8
Laos	-	-	-	-
Malaysia	7	6	11	5.9
Myanmar	4	8	7	3.9
Philippines	14	19	24	5.8
Thailand	1	1	1	11.5
Vietnam	1	2	3	10.1
Total	99	112	129	6.5

Table 4. Total consumption of pig meat and products in South-East Asia (kg/yr) (FAO, 1991)

Country	1980	1985	1990	Annual growth rate (%)
Cambodia	8	27	35	17.2
Indonesia	127	215	305	9.7
Laos	41	52	53	2.5
Malaysia	136	154	213	4.3
Myanmar	79	83	90	0.2
Philippines	413	397	666	4.2
Thailand	267	377	336	3.0
Vietnam	292	559	900	8.8
Total	1363	1710	2488	6.2

Table 5. Total consumption of poultry meat and products in South-East Asia (kg/yr) (FAO, 1991)

Country	1980	1985	1990	Annual growth rate (%)
Cambodia	10	17	24	10.1
Indonesia	177	329	496	11.3
Laos	10	19	25	8.7
Malaysia	140	242	347	11.9
Myanmar	68	109	90	2.2
Philippines	226	190	292	0.1
Thailand	327	420	506	4.1
Vietnam	145	150	161	2.1
Total	1103	1295	1629	6.3

Table 6. Total consumption of whole milk in South-East Asia (kg/yr) (FAO, 1991)

Country	1980	1985	1990	Annual growth rate (%)
Cambodia	14	16	16	1.4
Indonesia	316	412	507	5.4
Laos	6	8	35	16.5
Malaysia	217	160	214	-3.9
Myanmar	181	315	274	4.2
Philippines	175	149	412	7.6
Thailand	78	188	256	11.0
Vietnam	45	52	62	3.6
Total	1032	1300	1776	5.7

Table 7. Total consumption of eggs and products in South-East Asia (kg/yr) (FAO, 1991)

Country	1980	1985	1990	Annual growth rate (%)
Cambodia	7	10	14	8.2
Indonesia	215	303	408	7.1
Laos	20	25	29	3.4
Malaysia	87	104	148	6.1
Myanmar	31	50	33	0.9
Philippines	244	226	317	2.1
Thailand	161	194	191	1.6
Vietnam	90	112	139	4.9
Total	768	921	1131	4.2

Appendix 4

Table 1. Estimated quantities of cereal straws produced in South-East Asia (million tonnes) (FAO, 1989)

Country	Cereal straw*					Total	Contribution (%)	Total ruminant livestock units (RLU)**	Availability / RLU (million T)
	Maize	Millet	Rice	Sorghum	Wheat				
Cambodia	0.2	-	2.1	-	-	2.3	1.6	21.9	0.1
Indonesia	12.6	-	43.6	-	-	56.2	38.8	11.7	4.8
Laos	0.1	-	1.2	-	-	1.3	0.9	1.7	0.8
Malaysia	0.1	-	1.7	-	-	1.8	1.3	0.7	2.6
Myanmar	0.5	0.2	13.6	-	0.2	14.5	9.9	-	-
Philippines	9.0	-	9.5	-	-	18.5	12.7	24.2	0.8
Thailand	8.9	-	21.3	0.4	-	30.6	21.0	10.9	2.8
Vietnam	1.8	-	18.1	0.1	-	20.0	13.8	5.3	3.8
Total	33.2	0.2	111.1	0.5	0.2	145.2	100.0	76.4	2.0
Contribution (%)	22.9	0.1	76.6	0.3	0.1	100.0			

* Calculated using the grain:straw ratios of 1:1 for millet, rice and wheat, and 1:2 for maize and sorghum.

**Ruminant livestock units (RLU): buffalo = 1.0; cattle = 0.8; goat = 0.1; sheep = 0.1

Table 2. Availability of by-products from field crops in South-East Asia ('000 tonnes) (FAO, 1989)

Country	Castor bean meal	Cassava		Cotton seed meal	Maize germ meal	Rice		Sugarcane		Total availability	As % of total production
		leaves	Waste			broken	husk	bagasse	green tops		
Cambodia	0.5	16.7	23.2	0.4	19.6	94.5	357.0	29.7	38.5	580.1	0.9
Indonesia	-	1160.0	3495.2	2.6	1075.1	54.0	7406.0	3296.2	4272.8	20761.9	31.6
Laos	-	7.1	19.8	4.3	0.3	54.9	207.4	15.5	20.1	329.4	0.5
Malaysia	-	28.0	84.3	-	5.8	76.4	288.5	189.0	245.0	917.0	1.4
Myanmar	-	4.0	12.6	23.4	45.9	611.1	2308.8	121.9	542.5	3670.2	5.6
Philippines	0.9	129.2	396.7	3.0	768.7	425.7	1608.0	2374.8	3078.4	8785.4	13.3
Thailand	23.9	1643.2	4945.4	28.9	757.5	958.5	3621.0	4950.0	6416.9	23345.3	35.7
Vietnam	2.3	203.0	611.3	2.6	153.0	814.5	2986.0	789.8	1023.8	6586.3	11.0
Total	27.6	3191.2	9588.5	65.2	2825.9	3089.6	18782.7	11766.9	15638.0	64975.6	100.0

Table 3. Availability of by-products from tree crops in South-East Asia ('000 tonnes) (FAO, 1989)

Country	Cocoa		Coffee by-products	Oil palm			Rubber seed meal*	Total	As % of total production
	bean waste	pod husks		palm press fibre	kernel cake	mill effluent (dry)			
Indonesia	4.0	25.5	273.0	870.0	29.0	29.0	1066.1	2296.6	28.1
Malaysia	11.5	101.3	3.5	3044.2	101.4	101.4	1148.9	4512.2	55.2
Philippines	0.7	4.7	109.2	14.7	0.4	0.4	43.3	173.4	2.1
Thailand	-	-	10.5	80.4	2.7	2.6	922.6	1018.8	12.3
Vietnam	-	-	3.5	-	-	-	210.8	214.3	2.3
Total	16.2	131.5	399.7	4009.3	133.5	133.4	3391.7	8155.3	100.0

* Calculated from the land area under mature rubber in 1987 and the assumption that average seed production from mature rubber trees was 1000 kg/ha/year (de Padirac, 1987)